D1119188

Reading & Critical Thinking

Book 1

by **D**onald L. **B**arnes, Ed.D.
and **A**rlene **B**urgdorf, Ed.D.

Caleb E. Crowell, Editorial Director

ISBN# 0-87694-237-0 EDI 329

EDUCATIONAL DESIGN, INC.   **EDI 329**

Table of Contents

A. **L**iteral **R**eading **S**kills
B. **I**nferential **T**hinking **S**kills
C. **E**valuative **T**hinking **S**kills

This book is about two things—reading and thinking. These two things are really one. Thinking makes it possible for you to understand what you read. The better your thinking skills, the better you can read. This book will help you sharpen your reading and thinking skills.

The first ten chapters in this book concentrate on three groups of skills. They are Literal Reading Skills, Inferential Thinking Skills, and Evaluative Thinking Skills.

Literal Reading Skills are the ones you use to understand the basic meaning of what you read. The beginning chapters give you practice on three of the most important: how to figure out the meaning of unfamiliar words, how to keep track of events in a story, and how to spot and remember important details.

Inferential Thinking Skills go a step further. "Inferential" means "inferring"—that is, making a good guess. When you infer something, it means that you have reasoned that something is true without actually being told. Five chapters concentrate on these thinking skills, which are vital to a full understanding of what you read.

Evaluative Thinking Skills are the ones you use when you form opinions and make decisions. You use these skills when you compare one idea with another. Telling the difference between a fact and an opinion in a piece of writing is an evaluative skill. So is spotting the author's point of view.

Each of the first ten chapters in this book is organized the same way. The chapter begins with an explanation of what the skill is and contains some practice exercises for you to work with. Then come three stories with questions to give you understanding and practice on the skill. When you have completed these chapters, you will be able to handle the more difficult stories that follow.

1. Context and Word Meaning

Before you can start thinking critically about what you read, you have to understand the meaning of the words you are reading. But in your reading, you will often come across words whose meanings you do not know. What's the best way to figure out the meaning of a new word? Do you always need to get out a dictionary and spend time looking the word up?

Fortunately, there is another way that often works. You may be able to figure out the meaning of a word from its **context** — that is, by looking carefully at the rest of the sentence or at the sentences around it, and seeing how the word fits in.

Suppose, for example, you are told that someone has used **legumes** to prepare a vegetable soup. By looking at the context of the word "legumes," you can easily guess that legumes are some kind of vegetable. This meaning for "legumes" fits in best with the context of the rest of the sentence.

Everybody uses this "context clue" method of finding the meanings of new words quite naturally. In fact, you probably learned most of the words you know this way. But you use this method most often on spoken words. This is because when you hear a new word being spoken, you also hear the rest of the sentence. And you get the full context of the word.

When you **read** an unfamiliar word, however, you may tend to give up right there. And you may skip over the entire sentence in which it occurs. As a result you miss the context that might have given you a clue to the meaning.

The paragraphs below will give you practice in using context clues to figure out the meaning of unfamiliar words. Read each sentence carefully, especially if you don't know the meaning of the underlined word. And even if you do know the meaning of one of these words, look carefully at its context anyway. Notice how the context would help someone who didn't know the word's meaning.

At the end of each paragraph, you will find several possible meanings for the underlined words. Use the context of the paragraph itself to help you guess which meaning is correct.

King Tutankhamen, or King Tut, lived in ancient Egypt about 3,200 years ago. Although he was probably not an important king, the discovery of his tomb in 1922 was a very important event. The **excavation** of the tomb showed to the world for the first time how treasures were buried with the ancient Egyptian **pharaohs.**

1. In this paragraph, the word **excavation** seems to mean

    a. digging up
    b. sealing off
    c. repairing

2. In this paragraph, the word **pharaohs** seems to mean

   a. treasure
   b. kings
   c. tombs

Archeologist Howard Carter had been searching through Egypt's Valley of the Kings for years. This was where the tombs of other ancient Egyptian kings were located. The tombs that had been found earlier, however, had been **ravaged** by thieves. King Tut's tomb was the first to be found completely sealed.

3. In this paragraph, the word **archeologist** seems to mean

   a. a king
   b. a scientific explorer
   c. a thief

4. In this paragraph, the word **ravaged** seems to mean

   a. wrecked
   b. built
   c. sealed

When Carter and his team of archeologists opened King Tut's tomb, they found the mummy of the boy king. The body had **deteriorated,** so they couldn't tell much about the king himself. The **embalmers** who had prepared the body for burial had probably made an error. However, beneath the wrappings on the body were 143 pieces of ancient jewelry made of gold and precious stones.

5. In this paragraph, the word **deteriorated** seems to mean

   a. saved
   b. decayed
   c. moved

6. In this paragraph, the word **embalmers** seems to mean

   a. thieves
   b. workers who build pyramids
   c. workers who prepare the dead for burial

King Tut's body was returned to his **crypt,** but the treasures were placed in the Cairo Museum. The Tut treasures are occasionally loaned for exhibits in other countries. From 1977 to 1979 these golden **relics** were displayed in museums in major American cities.

7. In this paragraph, the word **crypt** seems to mean

   a. tomb
   b. museum
   c. wrappings

8. In this paragraph, the word *relics* seems to mean

   a. ancient objects
   b. digging tools
   c. bodies

In the story about Mt. Rushmore, there are additional words to figure out. See how well you can do.

The world's largest sculptures can be found on Mt. Rushmore in South Dakota. Carved on the side of the mountain are the *images* of four Presidents of the United States. They were carved over a period of 14 years. This monument is a truly *colossal* achievement! Sculptor Gutzon Borglum had to blast a million tons of rock from the top of the mountain before he could even start sculpturing the faces.

9. In this paragraph, the word *images* seems to mean

   a. stories
   b. faces
   c. remains

10. In this paragraph, the word *colossal* seems to mean

   a. huge
   b. weird
   c. tiny

Gutzon Borglum did not live to see the *culmination* of his work. He died just a few months before the *memorial* was completed. His son, Lincoln, who had worked along with his father, completed the project.

11. In this paragraph, the word *culmination* seems to mean

   a. picture
   b. completion
   c. beginning

12. In this paragraph, the word *memorial* seems to mean

   a. story
   b. monument
   c. job

Answers: 1. a, 2. b, 3. b, 4. a, 5. b, 6. c, 7. a, 8. a, 9. b, 10. a, 11. b, 12. b.

FROG AGAINST BAT

From Mexico to southern Brazil, scientists have found large bats that eat frogs. These bats locate frogs when the frogs are calling to their mates. The frogs have a real problem. They must somehow attract mates but not lose their lives to bats in the process. Bats, too, face a *dilemma.* They must learn how to locate frogs but avoid the poisonous ones — for some Latin American frogs are deadly.

To protect themselves, the frogs have learned to *vary* their calls. A complicated call to a mate is changed to a whine if frogs sense that bats are near. The frogs stop calling immediately when a large frog-eating bat flies overhead. But they do not interrupt their courting for a small insect-eating bat. Usually, frogs can tell the difference in the size of the bats. But on cloudy nights, when *visibility* is poor, they cannot distinguish between the various kinds of bats.

Bats, on the other hand, are able to tell the difference between complicated frog calls and more simple calls. They respond more *readily* to the regular mating call. Bats apparently are able to avoid poisonous frogs and toads through the use of special sensing equipment. Small, sensitive humps around the bat's mouth, called dermal denticles or "skin teeth," may warn them that a frog is poisonous.

Nature appears to have *furnished* both frogs and bats with a means of avoiding danger. In the frogs, changed or muted calls, *keen* sight, and sometimes poison have helped provide protection. In the bats, a keen sense of hearing and dermal denticles seem to allow them to find edible frogs and avoid poisonous ones.

QUESTIONS

Look at the words in italics in the sentences below. After each sentence, choose the word that means the same thing as the italicized word.

1. Bats face a *dilemma* because they must avoid the poisonous frogs.

    a. problem
    b. frog
    c. poison
    d. mate

2. The frogs have learned to *vary* their calls so the bats won't understand them.

    a. stop
    b. loud
    c. change
    d. begin

3. Frogs cannot distinguish between bats when *visibility* is poor.

    a. smelling conditions
    b. hearing conditions
    c. seeing conditions
    d. tasting conditions

4. *Keen* sight helps the frogs see bats at night.

    a. very bad
    b. very small
    c. very quiet
    d. very good

5. Nature *furnished* frogs with poison to protect themselves.

    a. supplied
    b. treated
    c. taken away

6. Bats respond more *readily* to regular frog mating calls.

    a. sadly
    b. quickly
    c. forcefully
    d. slowly

MINCEMEAT SWALLOWED WHOLE

"Operation Mincemeat" took place during World War II, in the spring of 1943. By that time the tide of battle was beginning to turn against Nazi Germany. A German army that had once numbered 285,000 had been destroyed at Stalingrad in Russia. And the *Axis* troops had surrendered in North Africa.

The *objective* of the Allies was to get from North Africa to Sicily without letting the Germans know where their landings would take place. They hoped to convince the Germans that they would be coming ashore at another location. Lieutenant Ewen Montague *devised* the plan to fool the Germans. He suggested using the body of a dead soldier. The body, carrying fake documents about a fake landing, would be taken to Spain to throw the Germans off the track. Spain was chosen because it was pro-German, even though it was not at war. The Spanish authorities would be sure to turn over any Allied secrets to the Germans.

The body of a pneumonia victim was used, and it was dressed to look like that of a British officer. The body, plus a sealed briefcase carrying the fake documents, was dropped overboard in the sea to wash ashore at the Spanish town of Huelva. In time, the British Army was informed that the Spaniards had recovered the body and buried it. There was no mention made of the briefcase which accompanied the body.

Immediately, the British pretended to be worried about the missing briefcase. A large number of messages were passed back and forth between Spanish and British authorities. After some days the briefcase was handed over.

After learning that the seals had been *tampered* with, the British flashed this message to the Prime Minister, Winston Churchill: *"Mincemeat Swallowed Whole."* The Germans had *intercepted* the misleading information. And they weakened their defenses in the very areas where the landings eventually took place.

QUESTIONS

Look at the words or phrases in italics in each of the sentences below. After each sentence, circle the letter of the word that means the same thing as the italicized word.

1. The **Axis** troops had surrendered in North Africa.

   a. English
   b. American
   c. German
   d. Spanish

2. Ewen Morgan **devised** a plan.

   a. developed
   b. stole
   c. used
   d. borrowed

3. The **objective** of the Allies was to fool the Germans.

   a. protest
   b. goal
   c. army
   d. anger

Circle the letter of the word that makes sense in each statement.

4. Someone had _____ with the lock on my door.

   a. hampered
   b. tampered
   c. sampled
   d. speckled

5. During the football game, the pass was _____.

   a. antiseptic
   b. intervarsity
   c. interviewed
   d. intercepted

6. In this story, the phrase **"Mincemeat Swallowed Whole"** means that _____

   _____

WILD-ANIMAL VETERINARIAN

Forty feet above the sun-baked ground, a man hangs from straps at the open door of a helicopter. He levels his sights on a galloping zebra. "Let 'er have it, Doc," shouts the pilot. There is a crack. Then a speck of blue appears on the right **haunch** of the animal near the tail. Soon the animal falls over.

Is this a new way to rid Africa of wild animals? No. It is a wild-animal veterinarian helping relocate animals to an animal park. A group of men in a truck soon appear and lift the zebra into a wooden crate. A short time later, the animal is injected with an *antidote,* and she is on her feet again.

The pair quickly take off in the helicopter. They are thankful that their work has been completed without injury to the animal. Almost at once, they pass over another herd of zebras. The animals approach a stand of trees and split. Moments later a *foal* rams into a tree and drops to the ground. The herd speeds on. "Land!" cries the vet. The helicopter is already on its way down.

The foal is alive but stunned. A quick examination reveals why it galloped into the tree. It is almost blind in both eyes. The small, struggling animal is quickly *sedated* and loaded into the helicopter. At Nairobi it is placed in a stall with a young assistant to watch over it.

The next day the vet prepares the foal for surgery. Medication is placed in the eyes. Two days later the eye operation takes place. In 20 minutes one eye is fixed. The other eye takes another 20 minutes. *Antiseptic cream* is put in both eyes to prevent infection, and the foal is carried to a dark stall.

Three days later the stitches are removed. The foal is put in with other zebras. It bounds around, stopping short of the fence and giving every indication of having good eyesight. Everyone involved, including the little patient, seems delighted with the outcome of the operation.

QUESTIONS

There are five words in italics in the story about the wild-animal vet. See if you can identify the correct meanings of these words by searching for clues within the same sentences and sentences surrounding the unfamiliar words. You may also find clues in other paragraphs.

1. In the first paragraph, we have the word *haunch.* We know that the zebra is running away from the helicopter, and we are also told that the haunch is near the tail.

   With these clues in mind, we can guess that *haunch* means

   a. foot
   b. neck
   c. hip
   d. head

2. You might substitute one of the following words for the word *haunch:*

   a. rump
   b. neck
   c. back
   d. foot

1. CONTEXT AND WORD MEANING

3. In the second paragraph, we find the word **antidote.** We know from the paragraph before that some kind of substance was shot into the zebra to knock it out. Now we find that an antidote has been given, and she is on her feet again.

   With these clues in mind, we can guess that an **antidote** is probably

   a. a shot to kill her
   b. a drug to counteract the first medicine
   c. a drug to fight infection
   d. a medicine to make her wild

4. You could substitute one of the following words for the word **antidote:**

   a. remedy
   b. poison
   c. sedation
   d. food

5. In the third paragraph, we find the word **foal.** If we glance at the next paragraph we find that the **foal** is called a small animal. Since this foal is running with the zebras, it is probably a zebra also.

   With these clues in mind, we can guess that **foal** means

   a. young zebra
   b. sick zebra
   c. hurt zebra
   d. odd zebra

6. You could substitute one of the following words for the word **foal:**

   a. old zebra
   b. baby zebra
   c. crippled zebra
   d. frightened zebra

7. In the fourth paragraph, we find the word **sedated.** We are told that the zebra ran into a tree and was struggling. The men want to help it, and they want to load it into the helicopter. It was **sedated** before they loaded it.

   With these clues in mind, we can guess that **sedate** probably means

   a. kill
   b. calm with medicine
   c. cure an injury
   d. tie the animal up

8. You could substitute one of the following words for the word **sedated:**

   a. cured
   b. lifted
   c. quieted
   d. let loose

9. In the fifth paragraph, we find two words, *antiseptic cream.* We know what cream is, but this is a special kind. It mentions that it is used to fight infection.

With these clues in mind, we can guess that *antiseptic cream* probably means

a. a cream that darkens the eyes
b. a cream that closes the eyes
c. a cream that fights germs
d. a cream that brightens the eyes

10. You could substitute one of the following words for *antiseptic cream:*

a. germ-fighting cream
b. greasy cream
c. calming cream
d. whitening cream

2. Sequence – The Order of Events

Morning comes before noon, and noon before afternoon. Spring comes before summer, and autumn follows. In real life — and in writing as well — events take place in a certain order, or sequence.

Understanding the sequence of events, whether in real life or in a piece of writing, is a key skill in understanding the events themselves. For example, writers of instructions may put their instructions in a particular sequence because that is the order in which they have to be done. Thus, the step-by-step instructions in a cookbook have to be followed in sequence. In making a cake, you have to mix the flour and milk before you put them in the oven, otherwise, there will be no cake.

Story writers, too, almost always put story happenings in a sequence. There is a beginning, a middle, and an ending. And there are also sequences of events within chapters and paragraphs.

In describing a sequence of events, it sometimes helps to think of the events in a stairstep arrangement, as shown below. Using this method, story details about a trip might be shown as follows:

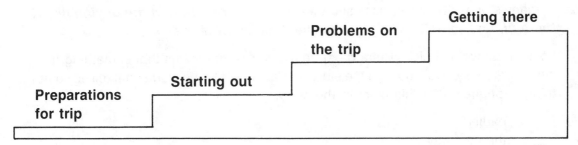

A story about a fire in a house might be shown this way:

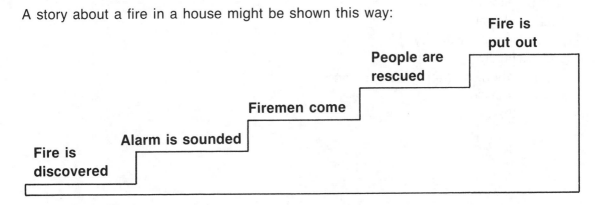

See if you can group the events of the story below in a stairstep sequence.

Bill Thompson first heard of the dreaded monster known as the Jersey Devil when he visited central New Jersey. None of the local people had actually seen the creature, but they had heard it roar at night. Thompson decided to try to capture it. He got together a large group of men. They were soon crisscrossing the woods looking for clues. Some of the men climbed trees and used powerful searchlights. On the fourth night, Thompson thought he heard a suspicious sound behind some trees. He walked toward it into the darkness, and was never seen again.

1. Now rearrange the events listed below to put them in sequence. Write the order of the events on the steps. You can use the letter before each event instead of writing it out in full.

   a. Thompson organizes a group of men
   b. Thompson disappears
   c. Thompson hears of the Jersey Devil
   d. Thompson hears a suspicious sound
   e. People hear the Devil roar at night
   f. Thompson searches the woods
   g. Thompson walks into the darkness

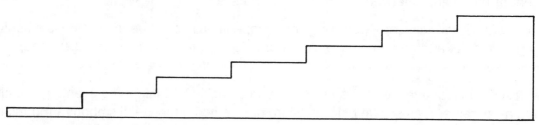

2. In many stories, the writer uses such words as **before, after, in the beginning, at the end,** and so on to help us understand the order of events.

   Look at the words below. Put a **b** before the words that tell us that something happened before a certain point in the story. Put an **a** next to the words that tell us something happened after this point in the story.

   _____ earlier
   _____ the next day
   _____ later
   _____ at first
   _____ as time went by
   _____ finally
   _____ when everything was finished
   _____ previously
   _____ then

SMOKE JUMPERS

People have been parachuting out of airplanes to fight forest fires since 1940. Today hundreds of these parachutists, called smoke jumpers, are on call throughout the West. The Forest Service employs about 360 jumpers in the Pacific Northwest. There are about 75 more in Alaska. The various jump centers are linked by computer. When a fire is spotted by a lookout, one of the centers is called. Often 8 to 12 men are in a plane and on their way within ten minutes. The plane reaches the fire site and drops the jumpers. As soon as they land, they gather up their chutes. They then scrape an 18-inch path completely around the blaze. This will hold the fire if the wind isn't too strong. Next, dead trees that might fall and spread the blaze are cut down.

Smoke jumping is different from other kinds of parachuting. Regular chutists, of course, avoid burning areas; smoke jumpers must purposely parachute into fire-ravaged regions. In addition, jumps are regularly made in areas along the ridges of six- to seven-thousand-foot-high mountains. This means that the air is quite thin. The parachutists usually come down very rapidly.

Between jumps, the crews continue to train. They also work at clearing trails and checking the forests.

People become smoke jumpers for many reasons. They may need a job. They may love the excitement of parachuting. In one fire season, a parachutist may jump as few as nine times or as many as 20. Jumpers often stay on because of the comradeship within the group.

QUESTIONS

1. Smoke jumpers often follow certain steps in fighting fires. Place numbers in the blanks below to show these steps. Steps 1, 5, and 8 are done for you.

   _____ A call is made to a jump center.
   _____ The smoke jumpers get on the plane.
   _____ The smoke jumpers leave the plane.
   __8__ The smoke jumpers dig an 18-inch path around the fire.
   _____ The smoke jumpers gather up their chutes from the ground.
   __5__ The plane flies over the fire site.
   _____ A plane is prepared for takeoff.
   __1__ A fire is spotted by a lookout.

2. Look over the events as they were explained in the story. Then cross out one of the words between parentheses ( ) to make each statement correct.

   a. Men parachuted from planes (before, after) 1940.
   b. Dead trees are cut out of fire areas (before, after) an 18-inch path is made around the fire.
   c. The plane flies over the fire site (before, after) the lookout calls the center.
   d. Chutes are gathered up from the ground (before, after) the smoke jumpers start fighting the fire.

THE RUNAWAY POND

June of 1810 was very dry near Glover, Vermont. Miller Aaron Wilson had only a bare trickle of water to power his waterwheels. His thoughts turned to nearby Long Pond, a mile and a half in length, three quarters of a mile wide, and 100 feet deep. Why not use pond water to run his mill?

Wilson talked with neighbors about the project. At 8 o'clock on a June morning, 50 men and boys trudged the five miles to the pond's northern rim. Their plan was to cut a small channel from the pond to the mill. First they hacked away cedar underbrush. Then they dug a shallow downhill trough. Near noontime, the last barrier between trough and pond was cut, and the water gurgled out. It was time for some lunch.

But lunch didn't last long. A yell came from the direction of the pond, and the men hurried toward it. They found one of their number, Spencer Chamberlin, up to his neck in quicksand. Within seconds, a swirling hole 60 feet deep and nearly as wide opened in the treacherous sand.

The men pulled Chamberlin out and scrambled for safety. One man went downstream to warn settlers below. Rushing water from Long Pond knocked down a grove of trees and soon reached Wilson's sawmill and flour mill. Both were demolished. The water continued, wiping out several bridges on the Barton River and destroying at least one more mill. It swallowed up whole herds of livestock, wild animals, and gardens. A 100-ton boulder was picked up and carried a mile. Cabins vanished and wagons were reduced to kindling.

In only four hours, the rampaging waters traveled the 20 miles to Lake Memphremagog and raised the waters of that huge lake a full foot. Yet, in spite of all the destruction, not a single human life was lost.

QUESTIONS

1. Listed below are the steps Wilson and his men followed to change the flow of the pond water. Place numbers in the blanks to put them in the proper sequence.

    _____ They dug a shallow trough.
    _____ A final barrier was cut, and the water poured out.
    _____ They cut away the thick underbrush.

2. Certain words often give clues to help us figure out the sequence in which story events take place. Decide whether each of the words listed below would appear at the beginning, middle, or end of a series of events. Then place the letter of the correct answer in the blank at the left of the word.

    _____ finally   a. beginning b. middle c. end
    _____ first   a. beginning b. middle c. end
    _____ continued   a. beginning b. middle c. end

3. The men found one of their number in quicksand

    a. after the water reached Lake Memphremagog
    b. before Wilson decided to reverse the flow of the pond
    c. after they cut the last barrier to change the flow of the pond water

4. Which of the following events took place *after* the men changed the flow of the water? (Choose one or more.)

    a. A 100-ton boulder was carried by the water for a mile.
    b. One man was sent to warn the settlers of the rushing water.
    c. The men walked the five miles to the pond at 8 A.M.
    d. Wilson's mills were destroyed.

5. The story describes the path the rushing water took through the countryside. Which event below is out of order?

    a. The water knocked over a grove of trees.
    b. It reached Lake Memphremagog.
    c. Wilson's mills were demolished.
    d. Several bridges were destroyed.

6. The story gives us three times when events occurred. Write the letter of each event beneath the clock face that shows the time the event took place.

    a. The men found Chamberlin trapped in quicksand.
    b. The men started the five-mile hike to the pond.
    c. The runaway waters raised the water level of Lake Memphremagog.

      _____   _____   _____

SPACE SURVIVAL

If a human being were unprotected in the near-vacuum of space, he or she couldn't breathe. The body would swell up because water, turned to vapor under the skin, would not be able to escape. It is clear that without support systems, manned space flight would be impossible.

The main requirements for survival in space include oxygen at the proper level of pressure; supplies of food and water; and systems to control humidity, insure a comfortable temperature, remove harmful gases, and handle liquid and solid wastes.

To satisfy all these requirements, the smallest of spaceships — the spacesuit — has been designed. Besides containing needed oxygen, the spacesuit must be insulated to protect the body from the intense heat of the sun and the intense cold of space. There must also be protection from radiation.

The original designs of spacesuits were copied from deep-sea diving outfits. The first model was developed in 1930 to protect high-altitude balloonists. During World War II and in the 1950's, there was a new need for high-altitude equipment, and the suits were improved.

In 1958 NASA (National Aeronautics and Space Administration) was formed, and work on Project Mercury, America's first space program, began. The spacesuit created for it was, in reality, two suits. The inner one was made of rubber and contained the oxygen. The outer suit was made of a canvaslike fabric and was meant to protect the inner suit from damage. The astronauts entered the spacesuits through zippered openings. Helmets and gloves were mechanically attached.

Later improvements in spacesuits include a suit of underwear with cooling tubes and a backpack for cylinders of oxygen and water. Today spacesuits come in small, medium, and large sizes. Future suits may be made of other fabrics and may make use of new types of life-support systems.

QUESTIONS

1. This story outlines the history of the development of the spacesuit. Number each of the descriptions below according to the order in which they were designed. Use *1* for the earliest description of the spacesuit and continue through *3.*

    _____ an inner suit of rubber and an outer suit of canvaslike fabric
    _____ a suit with high altitude equipment
    _____ a suit with a backpack for cylinders of oxygen and water

2. Key words such as ***first, next, last*** often provide clues to a story's sequence of events. In the spaces below, write three key words from the story which help to sequence events.

    a. _____
    b. _____
    c. _____

3. Look at the following time line. In the blanks below, write a brief description of the spacesuit as it appeared at that time.

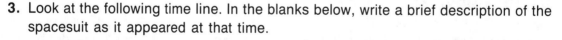

	A	B		C		D
	1945-1950	1958		1984		2000

a. _____

_____

b. _____

_____

c. _____

_____

d. _____

_____

4. In the pairs of descriptions below, circle the one that developed **after** the other.

a. Project Mercury . . . . space suits copied from diving suits
b. World War I . . . . the forming of NASA
c. suit designed to protect balloonists . . . . an inner suit of rubber and an outer suit
made of canvaslike material

3. Remembering Details

Sherlock Holmes, the famous fictional British detective, was the hero of 60 mystery stories. His clever observations and brilliant solutions often put the police inspectors from Scotland Yard to shame. Holmes saw and remembered tiny details. He would notice people's fingernails or their clothing. He would recognize their speech patterns. He would spot small objects at the scene of a crime. In the end, he was always successful in identifying the criminal.

Like Holmes, scientists study millions of details in their own work. Through very careful observations, some scientists have been able to discover and name almost 1,000,000 different creatures in the world. Even now, 7,000 to 10,000 additional insects are discovered each year.

Observing details is also important in reading and writing. Look at the sentence below. Read it. Now cover the sentence with your hand. Can you answer the questions that is asked below the statement?

> FINISHED FILES ARE THE RESULT
> OF YEARS OF SCIENTIFIC STUDY
> COMBINED WITH THE EXPERIENCE
> OF MANY YEARS.

How many times does the letter "f" appear in the sentence? _____
(If you wrote "three times," you are only half right. There are actually six "f's" in the sentence. Did you miss the three f's in the three "of's"?)

In many of the stories you read, you are given details about quantities or other numbers. Questions following the story may deal with these figures. You may be told, for example, that the sun is 93,000,000 miles from the earth. How can you remember a big number like 93,000,000? (Concentrate on the 93 separately from the millions.) People use different plans to remember. No matter what you decide to remember, decide first on the plan you will use to recall that detail.

Let's assume that you are trying to remember several details that are not quantities. You may want to *visualize* — that is, "to see" in your mind — what is being explained. The story below tells us about bacteria.

> Bacteria are tiny, one-celled organisms that can be found almost everywhere. They are found in deep oceans. They live in the air. They are also found in the soil.

You might visualize the details in the paragraph this way:

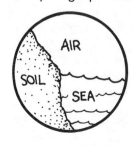

Bacteria help us to digest our food. They help us in preparing foods by causing fermentation. They also attack and destroy dead animals and plants. They help in purifying water. On the other hand, bacteria sometimes cause us to get sick. They also cause food to spoil.

The details here might be visualized as a chart this way:

GOOD	BAD
digest food	cause us to get sick
fermentation	
destroy dead animals and plants	cause food to spoil
purify water	

Visualizing the different ideas that are explained may help us recall important details. For example, we can immediately see that in this article bacteria are described as helpful in more ways than they are harmful.

Even if you are able to look back at what you have read, it helps if you have visualized or memorized important details. The understanding of details is a key part of understanding the story as a whole.

UTAH'S BAD MAN

One of the most famous of all Western outlaws, George LeRoy Parker, was born in 1866 in Beaver, Utah. He wasn't known by his real name, however. He adopted the name "Butch Cassidy." The "Cassidy" came from Mike Cassidy, who taught him rustling and horse thievery. "Butch" was acquired from a legitimate job he once had as a butcher.

Butch Cassidy began his cattle-rustling career in Utah. According to Butch's sister, he developed a kind of Robin Hood halo by never robbing "common people." He supposedly took only the illegal profits of bankers and cattle barons. This was not entirely true. He was not very careful about whom he robbed when he needed money.

In 1894 Butch was captured for the first and only time in his lawless career. He served a year and a half in jail. He then promised the governor of Wyoming that he would leave banks and livestock alone. He kept his word. He robbed trains instead!

Cassidy's gang, the Wild Bunch, flourished for a time, but the Pinkerton detectives soon began to close in. In 1901 Butch and his close friend, the Sundance Kid (Harry Longabaugh), decided to go to Bolivia in South America. They robbed the Bolivians until the two were supposedly killed by the Bolivian army in 1909.

There are several versions of how the two men died. None has been proved. Butch's sister wrote a book, published in 1976, entitled *Butch Cassidy, My Brother.* She says the two men killed in South America were intentionally misidentified so Butch could come home and start over. He died, she maintains, of pneumonia, in the fall of 1937.

QUESTIONS

1. In this story, Butch Cassidy is compared to

   a. the Lone Ranger
   b. Robin Hood
   c. Jesse James

2. Butch promised the governor of Wyoming that he would

   a. vote for him
   b. get a job
   c. stop robbing banks and cattle owners

3. Which three of the following details are **not** included in this story?

   a. Butch's sister wrote a book about her brother.
   b. Robert Redford starred in the movie "Butch Cassidy and the Sundance Kid."
   c. Butch was captured only once in his career.
   d. Butch once worked as a banker.
   e. Butch never married.

4. Most of the details in this story describe

    a. the life of famous western thief Butch Cassidy
    b. the Sundance Kid and his childhood
    c. horse thief Mike Cassidy

5. Butch's sister

    a. claimed he died of pneumonia
    b. hated him for his life of stealing
    c. visited him in jail after he was captured in 1894

6. Butch's partner in Bolivia was

    a. a Pinkerton detective
    b. Mike Cassidy
    c. the Sundance Kid

RAISING TROUT

Scientists have been growing baby fish to put into our lakes and streams for many years. Raising baby trout to a 5-inch size, however, is becoming very expensive. Each trout costs 60¢ to grow. It costs another 5¢ to transport it to a stream. Since millions of trout are grown, the costs are enormous.

There is now a cheaper and better way to hatch fish. The new method uses a device called a Vibert Box. This is a plastic container smaller than a cigarette package. It holds fertilized fish eggs in streams. The box was invented in 1950 by Richard Vibert, a French fisheries expert. The boxes were first used in Europe. They were introduced to this country in 1967. An improved version is now widely used.

Trout have traditionally been raised in special tanks by experts. The Vibert Box can be placed in streams by anyone. This saves the cost of many scientists. The improved version contains two parts — an incubator for eggs and a nursery for newly-hatched fry (young fish). The box is placed under coarse gravel in stream beds. Oxygen-containing water flows through slits in the box. The fry are safe from large fish until they can swim about on their own. Then they can swim out through small escape slots.

The Vibert Box has the advantage of hatching eggs in streams where the fish will eventually live. The tiny fish grow up already accustomed to the temperature and type of water of the stream. Vibert Boxes produce larger and stronger fish than the hatcheries do. The boxes hatch 95 out of 100 eggs, compared to 40 out of 100 in the hatcheries. The boxes cost only $2.00 each. This important invention may quickly replenish the streams of America.

QUESTIONS

1. See if you can visualize what the Vibert Box looks like. We are told that it is divided into two parts. Eggs are in one part. Slits let oxygen in for the eggs. Tiny fish (fry) are in the other part. They have slots so they can get out when they are strong enough to swim. Which picture below best fits the description of the box?

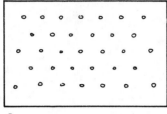
a.

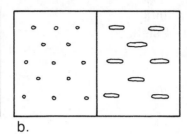
b.

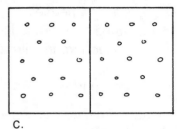
c.

2. Which details below appear in the story? (Check one or more.)

   a. Trout are using less oxygen today than they used to.
   b. The Vibert Box is being replaced by other devices.
   c. Fish do not like the Vibert Box.
   d. The Vibert Box has slots.

3. Trout have been traditionally raised in

   a. streams
   b. tanks
   c. rivers
   d. Vibert Boxes

4. The Vibert Boxes produce fish that are
   a. larger and stronger
   b. larger and happier
   c. easier to catch
   d. smaller but faster

5. The Vibert Boxes hatch

   a. 75 of each 100 eggs
   b. 40 of each 100 eggs
   c. 95 of each 100 eggs
   d. all of 100 eggs

6. The tiny fish in Vibert Boxes are accustomed to

   a. the temperature of the water
   b. each other
   c. riding in tank trucks
   d. scientists

7. Fish eggs are put in a Vibert Box and then placed

    a. in large tanks
    b. under coarse gravel in streams
    c. on the banks of streams
    d. on top of rocks in streams

8. The Vibert Box was first used in

    a. Africa
    b. South America
    c. Europe
    d. the U.S.A.

9. In this story, details were given about (Check one or more.)

    a. fishing for trout
    b. the use of the Vibert Box
    c. the life of Richard Vibert
    d. the advantages of using Vibert Boxes
    e. the problems in using Vibert Boxes

SEEING ALL OF THE WHITE HOUSE

John Zweifel was disappointed when he got to see only five rooms on his first public tour of the White House. He kept wondering what the other 127 rooms looked like. Now he knows, and so do many other people, because he has made a miniature White House that is 1/12th the actual size of the Presidential Mansion.

Zweifel is a designer of animated exhibits for department stores and theme parks. He began sketching, measuring, and photographing the White House in 1961 when the Kennedys granted him limited access to the Executive Mansion. Neither Johnson nor Nixon was interested in Zweifel's project and didn't help. But President Ford gave him almost unlimited access to the building. His research fills 300 files. With the help of his family, he has now constructed 45 tiny rooms showing the White House as it appeared in 1976.

The Zweifel White House measures 60 feet by 20 feet and weighs eight tons. It requires a 40-foot trailer when it goes on tour. Zweifel spent 150 days just carving the rosewood table in the Lincoln Sitting Room. He spent almost as long on the State Dining Room, which is set for 120 guests. The model is wired for electricity, its phones ring, its tiny television set flickers, and its small fountains spray jets of water.

Zweifel hopes his White House will be the centerpiece of the proposed White House Hospitality Center. In the meantime, work continues on the rest of the 132 rooms. The replica maker keeps up with the changes in room decoration initiated by new administrations. "Our warehouse," he jokes, "is getting bigger than the one storing furniture for the real White House."

QUESTIONS

1. According to the story, John Zweifel built his model of the White House because

   a. he knew the public would be willing to pay to see the model
   b. President Kennedy asked him to construct a model White House
   c. he didn't get to see all of the White House's rooms when he took a tour

2. Which of the following details is *not* included in the story? (Choose one or more.)

   a. Zweifel's White House model requires a trailer when it goes on tour.
   b. The model contains miniature phones that ring.
   c. President Nixon did not give Zweifel access to the White House.
   d. Zweifel was recognized by Congress for his detailed model.
   e. The White House consists of a total of 132 rooms.

3. In this story, most of the details describe

   a. the features of a model of the White House
   b. the offices of President Kennedy, President Johnson, and President Ford
   c. the White House hospitality center

4. Which three of the following details support the idea that Zweifel is a fine craftsman?

   a. He has 300 files filled with research on the interior of the White House.
   b. He spent 150 days carving a rosewood table for the miniature Lincoln Sitting Room.
   c. His family helped him build the model.
   d. Zweifel wired the miniature model for electricity.
   e. He began his work in 1961.

5. Zweifel's occupation is

   a. White House aide
   b. designer of department store exhibits
   c. carpenter

6. The story tells us that Zweifel

   a. completed 45 rooms and then stopped work on the model
   b. refused to finish the model after President Johnson said he wasn't interested in the project
   c. continues to work on the model

4. Identifying the Main Idea

Have you ever watched a small child learning to play baseball? He may strike out at bat but still run to first base. He may also hit the ball out into the field and remain standing at home plate. It usually takes a few days for him to really understand the *main idea* of the game.

When we read stories or reports, we also must look for the main idea. The main idea is the central point of the story. It is what the story is mostly about. Sometimes it is the lesson or moral of the story (as in a fable).

Read the paragraph below. Choose the statement following the paragraph that best states the main idea of the story.

> Jewell Johnson had lots of friends, but she liked Velma best of all. The two girls played ball together, went to movies, and even took trips together. One day Velma promised to help Jewell clean up after a party. Unfortunately, Velma forgot about her promise. Jewell ended up doing the whole job herself. She was so annoyed that she quarreled with Velma over her thoughtlessness. The two friends soon drifted apart.

1. The main idea of this story is:

    a. Friends are easy to find.
    b. Friends are important to everyone.
    c. A friend can be lost through thoughtlessness.
    d. Don't promise to help friends.
    e. Never clean up after a party with a friend.

It may be helpful to think of a main idea as an umbrella. Like an umbrella, the main idea is supposed to cover everything in the paragraph or story. All the details should fall under the umbrella of the main idea. If some of them do not fit under the main idea, we have picked the wrong statement for the major point of the story.

Statements which we select as main ideas for a story or a paragraph may be too broad, too narrow, or incorrectly stated. If a paragraph describes the habits of the swallow, it is likely that the word "swallow" will appear in the statement of the main idea. The main idea would not normally deal with *all* birds or *all* animals. Broadening the topic in this way is likely to make the statement of the main idea inaccurate and too sweeping.

See if you can select the statements that best represent the main idea of the stories below.

> Cicadas are large, dark insects with heavy bodies and thin wings. They are unusual because they spend most of their lives quietly underground.

> The female cicada starts her family by finding a twig. She makes a small hole in the twig with a sawlike organ near her abdomen. She places small eggs in this hole. In a few weeks, the eggs hatch into young cicadas, called nymphs. The nymphs drop to the ground and burrow holes. They attach themselves to roots. They remain there for 17 years feeding on the sap of the roots.

When the cicadas are full grown, something causes them to come to the surface of the ground. They climb up a tree, shed their outer coverings, and fly about. They feed and lay eggs.

2. Which of the statements below best represents the main idea of the story?

    a. Cicadas live underground.
    b. Cicadas can climb trees.
    c. Animals do peculiar things.
    d. Cicadas have an unusual life cycle.
    e. Cicadas are insects.

Read the story below about hyenas and label each of the statements following the story to indicate whether the sentences are too broad or too narrow to be the main idea.

The largest member of the hyena family is the spotted hyena. This doglike animal is often called the laughing hyena. The hyena doesn't laugh because of something funny or because it is tickled. It makes a laughing sound when it is excited and when it is seeking food. Since hyenas hunt at night, the laughing sound also allows the various members of a pack to keep in touch with each other.

Hyenas often eat what other animals have left behind. They wait until lions or other large animals have finished eating. Then they feed on the leftovers. But they also regularly chase and capture their own food.

3. Write "too broad" beside the statements that are too sweeping to be the main idea. Write "too narrow" beside the statements below that are just details. Put a check beside the statement that best represents the main idea:

_____ a. The spotted hyena is the largest hyena.
_____ b. The laughing and eating habits of the spotted hyena.
_____ c. Animals can be very funny.
_____ d. Hyenas eat leftovers.

Answers: 1. c, 2. d, 3. b. In Q. 3, a and d are too narrow, c is too broad.

LUXURY ON WHEELS

In 1908, "Old 16," an American Locomobile, roared across the finish line ahead of Italy's red Isotta. For the first time, the United States had won the International Cup race. The 1908 race was the fourth event of its kind; the previous three races were won by France.

The Locomobile was one of the finest cars ever manufactured in the United States. It was one of the most luxurious vehicles of the time. It was also the most expensive. It was made of heat-tested steel and weighed 4,800 pounds (800 pounds more than to-day's Lincoln Continental). In closed cars produced by Locomobile, the deep cushions were stuffed with horsehair, and the center light and cut-glass side lamps had expensive, colored-glass Tiffany shades. The trim was sterling silver, and there was even a telephone to talk to the driver!

The first Locomobiles were steam carriages, but by 1902 the company was producing two- and four-cylinder cars. They quickly became known for their power, speed, and reliability. Even in 1922, a six-passenger Locomobile cost $11,300, while the most expensive Cadillac was listed at $4,600. A good home at the time might sell for $3,500.

Locomobiles were strong and durable. General Pershing's Locomobile survived World War I and was bought by a private citizen at the end of the conflict. In 1953, this same car was driven from the east coast of the United States to Tulsa, Oklahoma, for an antique car meet. And as for "Old 16," it too still survives. It is now owned by Peter Helck, an illustrator who is known for his vivid paintings of car races.

QUESTIONS

1. This story mainly describes

   a. the 1908 International Cup Race
   b. General Pershing's command during World War I
   c. the American Locomobile

2. Which of the following is the main idea of paragraph 2?

   a. The Locomobile weighed over 4,000 pounds.
   b. The Locomobile was a luxurious vehicle in its time.
   c. The Locomobile was equipped with a telephone.

3. Which of the following would be the main idea for a paragraph describing the owners of Locomobiles?

   a. The Locomobile performed well under racing conditions.
   b. The Locomobile was certainly an expensive automobile to produce.
   c. The Locomobile attracted wealthy, luxury-minded consumers.

4. Which of the following sentences states the main idea of paragraph 4?

    a. Locomobiles were strong and durable.

    b. "Old 16" is now owned by Peter Helck, an illustrator who is known for his vivid paintings of cars.

    c. General Pershing's Locomobile survived World War I and was bought by a private citizen at the end of the conflict.

5. From the list below, place a check beside the three details that are *least* important to the story's main idea.

    a. The Locomobile was one of the most elaborate, expensive American automobiles.

    b. Locomobiles were known for power and speed.

    c. Peter Helck is a painter of car races.

    d. Locomobiles were strong and dependable.

    e. France won the first three International Cup races.

    f. Today's Lincoln Continental weighs approximately 4,000 pounds.

6. Of the possible story titles below, which would be the most suitable alternate title for this story?

    a. "Locomobile vs. Cadillac"

    b. "An Inferior Automobile"

    c. "Today's Car Industry"

    d. "The Locomobile's Elegant History"

CLOCKWORK BEES

The built-in time clocks that seem to govern the behavior of bees have interested many people. In the early 1900's, a Swiss doctor named Forel noticed that bees arrived in his yard at about the same time each morning. Later, around 1912, Karl von Frisch began serious work on the behavior of bees. His carefully designed investigations became world famous. At first von Frisch put out dishes of sugar, water, and honey at the same hour each day. He marked the bees that came. A timekeeper kept a record of each bee's arrival time. Even when no food was set out, the bees appeared at exactly the same time.

Ingeborg Beling, a student at the University of Munich, also trained bees to come at a particular time of the day. Next she tried to train them to come at 19-hour intervals. It didn't work. Then she tried to get them to come every 48 hours. That didn't work either. She concluded that the bees' sense of time depended on a circadian rhythm. (The word "circadian" means "about a day.")

It was clear that bees have a keen sense of time. The next question to be answered was, what makes the bees' clock work? Are their travels influenced by forces around them, such as weather and humidity? The bees were moved to a room inside a large building. The temperature, humidity, light, and air were kept constant. This didn't change the bees' schedule. Radiation from the sun was eliminated as a contributing factor by testing the bees in a dark tunnel. Again, there was no change.

The last experiment in which the bees were tested took place after World War II. It involved transporting them across the Atlantic Ocean in a plane. When it was 8:15 P.M. in Europe, the time was 3:15 A.M. in New York. The bees in Europe ate at their accustomed New York time (which corresponded to their old 24-hour schedule).

QUESTIONS

1. This story is mainly about

    a. a Swiss doctor's experiments with bees
    b. the process bees go through to make honey
    c. the internal time schedule of bees

2. In a paragraph about different scientists' studies of bees, which of the following would be an appropriate topic sentence for the paragraph?

    a. The beehive community is composed mainly of worker bees.
    b. Many experiments have been performed to discover why bees behave the way they do.
    c. To protect himself from bee stings, the scientist must wear protective clothing and a special hood.

3. Write out the main idea for each of the following paragraphs of the story:

    a. Paragraph 2: _____
    b. Paragraph 3: _____
    c. Paragraph 4: _____

For each of the topic sentences below, check the details in the list after it that would help to support the sentence in a paragraph.

4. Scientists have shown great interest in bee behavior. (Choose three.)

    a. In Berlin, a researcher examines the flight patterns of two swarms of bees.
    b. An experimenter studies beehive activity in three stages.
    c. Bees produce several hundred gallons of honey each year.
    d. A swarm of bees maintains a complex community within the hive.
    e. Two doctors record the migrating habits of a bee swarm.

5. Bee behavior is controlled by a built-in time clock. (Choose two.)

    a. Movies protraying "killer bees" have created unnecessary fear in some areas of the world.
    b. A doctor observes that bees appear in his yard at approximately the same time each day.
    c. Bees play a crucial role in nature by pollinating flowers and blossoms.
    d. The sting of a bee may be fatal to people who have allergic reactions.
    e. One researcher has discovered that the behavior of bees is determined by a circadian rhythm.

6. Which of the following would be a suitable alternative title for this story? (Choose one.)

    a. "Too Many Bees"
    b. "A Bee's Timeclock"
    c. "The Royal Queen Bee"
    d. "The Beekeeper's Job"

GIVE ME A HOME WHERE THE INSECTS ROAM

Would you like to have a home that you have built yourself? Would you like a home that is also a trap for your food? The spider seems to be quite content with this arrangement.

Before a spider builds its web, it must find two solid surfaces for support. It can use the corner of a house, two bushes, the inside rafters in barns, or any other supports that are approximately three feet apart. Outside locations over a grassy area where plenty of insects are flying and running are ideal.

When all is planned, including the testing of the wind, glands in the spider's abdomen produce a liquid. This liquid is forced through tubes called spinnerets at the rear of the spider's body. When the liquid is exposed to the air, it immediately hardens. The wind helps carry the strand to a nearby surface. The first strand forms a bridge on which the spider can travel. The spider then continues making strong threads for the web as well as sticky interior threads to trap prey.

When the work is finished, the spider waits for a visitor to fly by and get caught. As soon as an insect becomes tangled in the web, the spider weaves more strands around the helpless victim. It then bites the insect. The spider does not stick to its own web because it has oil on its feet. When it is wet outdoors, the spider's web doesn't work very well. It loses most of its stickiness.

The strands of silken thread which spiders use to make a living are also very important to people. Ever since the days of our nation's best-known surveyor, George Washington, experts in the field of optics have agreed that the strands of silken threads in a web are best for crosshairs in sighting instruments. "Black widow webs are best," says Charles Dilger of North American Supply Company. Their web provides the best combination of strength and thinness. Human hair is far too thick. It is 80 times the width of spider web strands. Nylon threads won't do either, because when nylon strands are magnified, surveyors are distracted by the fibers in it.

Since black widow spiders are very poisonous, care is taken in removing the filaments from them. When spider strands are needed, the black widow is placed in a small jar. A probe is used to tickle the spider on the tummy. When this occurs, it starts secreting strands. These are wound onto a fork. An active black widow can produce as much as two feet of webbing in a day.

QUESTIONS

Let's see if you can decide what the main idea is for each of the last five paragraphs in the story below.

1. What is the main idea of Paragraph 2?

    a. Why the spider builds a web is important.
    b. When the spider builds a web is not important.
    c. Where the spider builds a web is important.
    d. Grassy areas are best.

2. What is the main idea of Paragraph 3?

    a. The spider has a definite step-by-step way of building a web.
    b. The first strand forms a bridge.
    c. The spider's abdomen produces fluid.
    d. The wind helps carry the first strand.

3. What is the main idea of Paragraph 4?

    a. What the spider does when a victim becomes entangled in its web.
    b. The spider's feet don't stick to the web.
    c. Why the wetness outdoors makes the web less sticky.
    d. How the spider waits for its victim.

4. What is the main idea of Paragraph 5?

    a. Human hair is thicker than spider filaments.
    b. Black widow webs are best.
    c. The strands of thread which spiders make are used for crosshairs.
    d. Nylon threads have fibers in them.

5. What is the main idea of Paragraph 6?

    a. The black widow spider is poisonous.
    b. How the strands of thread are taken from black widow spiders.
    c. The black widow is placed in a jar.
    d. A probe is used to tickle the spider on the tummy.

5. Judging the Adequacy of Information

When writing a story, newspaper writers try to pack all the basic information into the first paragraph. To decide on what information is basic, they answer all the five WH questions (plus two questions beginning with H):

Who? — The main people involved in the story
What? — The story or event itself — what happened
When? — Time
Where? — Place
Why? — Reason
How? — The way in which something was done
How Much? — Any important quantities or amounts of money, time, weight, height, etc. — any important numbers in the story

A careful, thoughtful reader reading the story will be able to answer these five WH and two H questions. For example, look at this report:

Jim Robertson came to Frankfort in May. His dad had lost his job in California. Jim and his family loaded all of their belongings into a trailer behind the car. Going over the mountains took more time than they had expected. Jim and his family arrived in Frankfort five days after leaving their home in California.

This short report answers all of the key questions:
- Who — Jim Robertson and his family
- What — moved to a new town
- When — in May
- Where — from California to Frankfort
- Why — because Jim's dad lost his job
- How — by car and trailer
- How much — in five days' time

Being aware of the five WH (and two H) questions is a good way to focus your reading. If someone asks you what a story is about, you should be able to answer using the questions as a guide. And you should be able to spot whenever any of the questions are not answered in a story. For example, in the story below, Jose Garcia did not answer all of the key questions when he planned a contest. See if you can figure out which key questions Jose forgot to answer.

Jose Garcia had always been interested in model planes. His older brother had taught him how to make them. Jose had spent many hours building planes in his basement. He thought it would be fun to have a model plane contest. He planned to charge an entry fee and give prizes for the planes that flew the best. He asked all the boys who had planes to bring them to his house for a contest.

Jose was disappointed when the contest was a flop. The boys knew who was to come, where they were to go, what was planned, and why they were to bring their planes.

1. What had Jose forgotten to tell them? List at least two WH or H questions that Jose forgot.

a. _____

b. _____

Have you ever read about the Lost Colony of Roanoke? An English settlement had been established in the 1580's on Roanoke Island off the coast of what is now North Carolina. When a supply ship from England visited the island three years later, everyone had disappeared. The only clue left behind was the word "CROATOAN" carved on a tree.

Scientists have noted that there are 12,000 Croatan Indians living in North Caroliona today. They are not at all like other American Indians. The Croatans have light skin, blue or gray eyes, and English names. They speak a kind of English with sayings that have not been used in this country for over 300 years. Historians have suggested that the colonists have have intermarried with the original Indians, and these unusual Indians today are their descendants.

2. Match.

____ lost colony of Roanoke	a. Who
____ in the 1580's	b. What
____ off coast of what is now North Carolina	c. When
	d. Where
____ disappeared	

3. Match.

____ settlers and Croatan Indians	a. What
____ may have intermarried	b. Who
	c. Why
____ because present-day Croatan speech, names, and physical types suggest this	

BRITISH ESCAPE ARTIST

In 1899, the northern part of what is now the Republic of South Africa was under the control of descendants of Dutch settlers, known as Boers. When Great Britain and the Boers had a falling out, war broke out in 1899. Winston Churchill, then a 24-year-old journalist for the London *Morning Post,* was sent to South Africa as a war correspondent. Churchill joined infantry companies being transported on an armored train, and shortly afterward the train was captured by the Boers. Young Churchill was sent to a prisoner-of-war camp at the Boer capital of Pretoria.

While a captive, Churchill studied the prison. It was surrounded by ten-foot walls or fences, and Boer sentries were posted every 50 yards outside. Powerful floodlights lit the area, except for one dark section in the shadow of a small building. Churchill watched the guards. When two of them turned their backs at about the same time, he ducked into the shaded area and sailed over the fence. He was out!

Now he faced 300 miles of hostile Boer country before he could reach friendly Portuguese East Africa. He had no compass to let him know which way he was heading, nor did he speak Dutch, the language of the Boers. By hopping railroad cars for short distances and walking by night, he finally reached a coal mine where he decided he had to get help. Luckily, he knocked on the door of the only house for 20 miles around which had a British resident.

Arrangements were made with the British householders to accompany Churchill to the border. A reward had been offered for his capture. Churchill found his way through Portuguese territory and later returned to Britain as a hero. He went on to become one of Britain's greatest statesmen-politicians.

QUESTIONS

1. In the list below, check off three pieces of information that are presented in the story.

    a. Churchill was imprisoned in an African camp.
    b. Great Britain and the Boers went to war.
    c. Churchill became Britain's Prime Minister.
    d. He escaped from the prison camp by climbing over a fence.
    e. Churchill was a statesman at the time of the South African war.

2. Of the following pieces of information, which one is *least* important to the action of the story?

    a. Churchill was 24 when he was sent to Africa.
    b. Churchill freed himself from a prisoner-of-war camp.
    c. In Boer country, he luckily found the house of the only British native for 20 miles around.

3. In the third paragraph, the author tells you that Churchill lacked two things while traveling in the Boer country. What were they?

    a. _____

    b. _____

4. For each of the statements below, write one example of proof you would use to support the statement.

    a. In this story, Churchill was a lucky man. _____

    b. In this story, Churchill was a clever man. _____

    c. In this story, Churchill was a hero. _____

5. Which statement contains a valid cause-effect relationship?

    a. He escaped from the prison camp, and he became a great statesman.

    b. He found the home of British residents; he was able to reach the Portuguese border.

    c. Because a reward had been offered for his capture, Churchill made his way through Portuguese territory.

6. From the list below, choose the piece of information that is *not* presented in this story.

    a. Churchill published the story of his escape in the *New York Times.*

    b. British residents helped Churchill reach the Portuguese border.

    c. When he was sent to cover the story of the war, Churchill traveled with infantry companies.

THE HEADLESS GHOST

Most of the ghost stories we hear seem to have happened a long time ago. One ghost, however, came out of hiding as recently as 1982. It was seen in the Miramar Hotel in California.

Ann, a maid who had worked at the hotel for many years, was on her way through the basement. Suddenly she noticed a soldier walking in front of her. Just as quickly, he disappeared. There was only one way out of the hallway. This was up a stairway to the lobby of the hotel. It was closed by an iron gate. The gate reached from the floor to the ceiling. It was securely chained and locked.

The desk clerk said he had not seen the ghost. However, he would not go into the basement alone because several people had reported seeing a headless ghost wearing khaki pants and shirt. A maintenance worker admitted that he had seen the ghost. He had also heard doors slamming in the basement from time to time. Recently, another worker was painting a bed in the basement. He saw someone in a khaki uniform float by.

The hotel owner's secretary reports that when she goes to the basement she has the feeling that someone is watching her. Her boss has set up cameras throughout the basement. Unfortunately, he has not been able to get any pictures of the strange intruder.

The earliest sighting of the ghost was 20 years earlier. The hotel's chef was in the storeroom, and the ghostly soldier simply came out of the wall. She said he was in a khaki uniform and was floating through the air. She has seen the ghost since then at various times. One time he was in the elevator with her. He just walked through the elevator wall. She noticed that he had no head.

Is there a ghost in the Miramar Hotel? You'll have to decide for yourself.

QUESTIONS

Who, what, when, and where questions about the ghost. Check the best answer to each question:

1. Who was the first person to see the ghost?

   a. the hotel chef
   b. the desk clerk
   c. Ann, the maid
   d. the maintenance worker

2. Where has the ghost been seen most often?

   a. in the elevator
   b. in the basement
   c. near the hotel clerk
   d. in the kitchen

3. When does the ghost normally appear?

   a. at night
   b. the story doesn't tell
   c. during the day
   d. on the first of the month

4. What did the ghost look like?

   a. a tiny man
   b. a soldier
   c. a clown
   d. a woman

5. Let's assume that you want to prove that there really is a ghost at the hotel. What kinds of evidence would be most convincing? (Check the two best answers.)

   a. a statement from a fortune teller that ghosts do exist
   b. a photograph of the ghost in the hotel
   c. a recording of the ghost saying something
   d. a statement by a minister that lots of people believe in ghosts

6. Let's assume that you want to prove that the ghost at the hotel is a fake. What evidence would be most convincing?

   a. proof that soldiers didn't like the Miramar
   b. statements by a minister that many people don't believe in ghosts
   c. evidence that an old employee likes to pull practical jokes and to fool people

THE GREAT TEMPLE OF THE AZTECS

Mexican scientists have peeled away many layers of soil and broken stones in the heart of old Mexico City. Underneath they have found a fascinating maze of ancient buildings, passageways, and pyramids. The site was partially opened to the public in September, 1982, and has become one of the biggest attractions in ruins-rich Mexico.

The site is the size of a football field. It lies just off the Central Plaza in Mexico City. Tourists can view the native Aztec Indian culture that Cortez and his soldiers found when they first came to Mexico City in 1519. From the top of the temple, the ancient Aztec ruler, Montezuma, proudly showed Cortez the city extending for miles in all directions.

The temple stood 200 feet high and measured 250 feet on each side. The Spanish conquerors tore it down stone by stone. The process may have taken 14 years. For 450 years afterwards, it was forgotten. Then in February 1978, a ditchdigger working nine feet below ground level found a carved monolith (large block of stone used in buildings) and a sculpture of an Aztec goddess.

The ditchdigger's find triggered four years of full-scale digging by scientists from Mexico's National Institute of Archaeology. The scientists have uncovered a remarkable system of five interlocking pyramids in one area and temples built over earlier temples.

The Spaniards apparently overlooked the earliest, innermost, and smallest of the five temples. In two pyramids, shrines to the rain god Tlaloc and the wargod Huitzilopochtli remain almost untouched, including the anvillike stone on which humans were sacrificed to the gods.

The base of the grandest and last temple is decorated with carved stone figures of serpents and frogs. The scientists have also found 105 clay urns used for offerings as well as vases and stone basins that held more than 6,000 priceless objects from the Aztec age. By studying these temples and their contents, scientists can discover a great deal about the great civilization of the Aztecs.

QUESTIONS

1. Check off the three pieces of information below which are presented in the story.

   a. The Mayan civilization was more advanced than the Aztec civilization.
   b. In two of the pyramids, shrines to the gods Tlaloc and Huitzilopochtli were discovered.
   c. Montezuma was an Aztec ruler.
   d. The Spaniards destroyed the Aztec temple.
   e. Cortez murdered the Aztec ruler.

2. Which of the following statements gives proof to the statement "the Aztecs were a highly religious people"?

   a. The site is the size of a football field.
   b. Montezuma was proud of the building accomplishments of his people.
   c. Scientists have uncovered clay urns used for offerings, shrines, sacrificial stones, and the figurine of a goddess.

3. Which of the pieces of information below is *not* included in the story?

    a. Mexico's National Institute of Archaeology sold some of the Aztec artifacts to the United States.

    b. Tourists are allowed to view the ruins of the Aztec empire.

    c. One of the temples is decorated with carved serpents and frogs.

4. Full-scale excavating of the site began because

    a. A Mexican scientist discovered the remains of Cortez's diary, which told of the hidden artifacts.

    b. A ditch digger uncovered a carved monolith of an Aztec goddess.

    c. Scientists discovered the tomb of Montezuma.

5. If you were studying the civilization of the Aztecs, which of the types of information below would be most important to your study?

    a. the religious practices of the Aztecs

    b. the methods used by scientists in museums

    c. the rulers of Aztec government

    d. the buildings of Aztec cities

    e. businesses in modern Mexico

6. Which of the sentences below show probable cause-effect relationships? (Choose two.)

    a. Tourists can see the site because the Spaniards destroyed the temples.

    b. The Aztecs were a religious people; many of their statues are of gods.

    c. A ditch digger found a statue, and full-scale digging was started.

6. Citing Evidence

If you want to persuade or convince a friend that something you say is true, simply saying it is not enough. You also have to add information that supports what you say. Information like this, which tends to prove that something is true, is called **evidence.** Pointing out or describing the evidence that something is true is called **citing evidence.**

Suppose you want to persuade your friends that your dog is unusually clever, or that you have made a model airplane that flies in unusual patterns. Until you give examples and details about what you dog or airplane has done, your friends may not believe you. If you cite some evidence for your claims, they will be much more firmly convinced.

When we read stories or reports, we are also dealing with information and evidence. If two people read a story and come away with different ideas about the author's meaning or about the characters and events in the story, they can always go back and recheck the details. They can point to specific paragraphs, sentences, or words that support their ideas — or that do not support them.

Recognizing or finding evidence for the statements you read or for what you remember from your reading is one of the most important of all thinking and reading skills. If you work on this skill and develop it, you will be much better at understanding and remembering what writers are saying. And you will be better at finding evidence to form and to back up your own opinions.

Below is an opportunity to practice your ability to find evidence for different statements. It is a short story about the U.S. Camel Corps (a corps is a section of an army). The questions following the story will have you point out the evidence for various statements by citing the paragraph and sentence number where each piece of evidence appears.

¹Almost everybody knows that the U.S. Army once used horses. Not many people, however, know that the Army once had a Camel Corps. In 1850 we did not have a railroad from coast to coast. The Army, however, needed a quick, easy way of moving supplies in the dry southwestern part of the nation. These supplies were needed by Army troops fighting Indians in California, New Mexico, Arizona, and Colorado.

²An Army lieutenant, Edward Beale, suggested using camels. Congress voted $3,000 to buy the animals. They sent two officers to Italy and Africa to study camels and to purchase some for the Army. When the two officers arrived in Europe and learned that camels could carry 600-pound loads and travel 30 miles a day, they bought 33 of them. They also hired three drivers to help with the animals.

³At first, many cowboys laughed at the camels. Then they found out how strong and durable they were. They could travel for miles over rocks, deserts, and mountains. They could even swim across large rivers.

[4]Lt. Beale was made commander of the U.S. Camel Corps. He quickly set up supply routes to the forts farther west. The camels carried guns and ammunition, supplies of food, and equipment to the troops. But when horses smelled the camels, they ran away in terror.

[5]The United States Camel Corps worked very well until the Civil War broke out. When the war began, the troops in the West were called east. Some of the camels were turned loose. Some were given to the city of Los Angeles to carry mail and move goods back and forth from ships in the harbor. When railroads crossed the continent, the U.S. Camel Corps was soon forgotten.

QUESTIONS

1. When the cowboys first saw the camels, they were amused. What paragraph gives the evidence that made the cowboys change their minds?

   Paragraph number ____

2. Congress evidently though that Lt. Beale's idea was a good one. Congress did two things to get the camels for the Army. Where in the story are these actions by Congress described?

   Paragraph number ____   Sentences number____ and _____

3. The camels were not useful working alongside horses. What sentence gives evidence for this statement?

   Paragraph number ____   Sentence number ____

4. Where in the story do we learn about the value of the camels during the Civil War?

   Paragraph number ____

5. What evidence does the writer of the story give that the camels were tough?

   Paragraph number ____
   Paragraph number ____

Answers: 1. Paragraph 3. **2.** Paragraph 2 Sentences 2 and 3. **3.** Paragraph 4 Sentence 4. **4.** Paragraph 5. **5.** Paragraph 2, Paragraph 3.

THE ECCENTRIC INVENTOR

Most stories about Thomas Alva Edison tell about his inventions. But there was another interesting side to the great inventor — his unusual habits.

To be sure, he was a genius. He either invented or greatly improved the telephone, telegraph, typewriter, phonograph, mimeograph, electric light, motion picture projector, electric generator, storage battery, and more than 1,000 other devices.

But in spite of his success, he was very human. Edison had odd habits. He slept in his clothes because he believed that changing them or taking them off brought sleeplessness. He often nearly starved himself because he thought food poisoned his intestines. He lived on five hours of sleep a night during most of his life. When asked about exercise, he said, "I use my body only to carry my brain around."

Early in life, his interest in inventions got him into trouble. At the age of 15, he blew up a telegraph station while experimenting with a battery. At 16, while working for the railroad, he forgot to set out a danger signal and a train was derailed. And he started a fire in a baggage car with his experiments in chemistry. But despite these setbacks, he signed his first contract for an invention at 19.

Throughout his life, Edison believed in long, hard work. Yet when people remarked about how dedicated he was, he quickly pointed out that his efforts had a major purpose. "Anything that won't sell I don't want to invent," he said. Edison's ideas probably can be summed up in his statement, "Remember, nothing that's good works by itself. You've got to make it work."

QUESTIONS

1. Which two of the following pieces of evidence would support the statement, "Edison had odd habits"?

   a. Edison forgot to send out a danger signal when working for the railroad.
   b. Edison slept in his clothes.
   c. Edison devised ingenious inventions.
   d. Edison often starved himself because he feared poisoning.

2. Based on what you have learned from the story, which of the words below best describe Edison?

   a. hardworking
   b. ingenious
   c. sad
   d. angry
   e. unusual

3. The story tells us that Edison was a genius. Describe *two* pieces of evidence you would use to support that statement.

   a. _____

   b. _____

43

4. Edison said, "Anything that won't sell I don't want to invent." Using this statement as evidence, what could you say about Edison's attitude towards his work?

    a. He didn't care very much about his inventions.

    b. He thought it was important to be successful with his inventions.

    c. He didn't mind if people didn't buy his inventions; he just wanted to invent.

5. Which two of the following support the idea that Edison was sometimes careless while working on an invention?

    a. He invented the telephone, telegraph, and electric light.

    b. He signed his first contract at age 19.

    c. He blew up a telegraph station while experimenting with a battery.

    d. He forgot to send out a danger signal for the railroad.

6. The fact that Edison slept only five hours each night can be used as evidence to support which of the statements below?

    a. Edison believed in long, hard work.

    b. Edison was a great inventor.

    c. Edison was a genius.

CHINA'S WONDER WALL

No single picture, no quick visit, no short description can give a real idea of the size of China's Great Wall. It stretches 1,500 miles from the Pacific Ocean to the Gobi Desert. If transferred to the United States, it would stretch from Kansas to New York. Built to keep enemies out of China, it is estimated that the wall contains enough materials to make a barrier eight feet high and three feet thick around the globe at the equator.

Work on the Wall was begun about 300 B.C. In 221 B.C. Emperor Qin rose to power. He extended the Wall along the northern border of China. Later rulers erected fortifications. Its final segments were completed during the Ming Dynasty (1368-1644).

The Wall wanders across plains, valleys, mountains, and gorges. It loops, snakes, doubles back on itself, and puts out extensions for a total of 3,700 miles. On top of the Wall is a road on which five horses can walk side by side. Part of it is constructed of gray granite blocks that weigh two tons each. In places, these blocks were hauled to mountain ridges more than a mile high, apparently without the use of machinery!

Some sections of the Wall were constructed of earth and wood and topped with stone. And in the desert, the Wall was built with sand, pebbles, and twigs covered with mud brick. Much of this has deteriorated, but still standing are many of the 25,000 towers that dot the wall from one end to the other.

The Great Wall is the biggest thing that humans have ever built. Yet it was not a success. Over and over, northern enemies broke through and set up kingdoms in China. Nevertheless, the kingdoms are gone. The Wall still stands.

QUESTIONS

1. This story tells us that the Great Wall is one of man's most incredible engineering feats. Which three of the statements below support this idea?

   a. The Wall did not keep enemies out.
   b. The materials in the Wall could build a barrier stretching around the earth.
   c. The Wall runs from the Pacific Ocean to the Gobi Desert.
   d. A great deal of the wall has deteriorated.
   e. The builders of the Wall hauled two-ton granite blocks without machinery.

2. What evidence do we have in the story that tells us the Wall was built over a long period of time?

   _____

3. Which of the following pieces of evidence tells us that the Wall was built so that the Chinese soldiers could travel on it?

   a. Emperor Qin extended the Wall for 1,700 miles.
   b. The Wall goes over valleys and mountains.
   c. There is a road on top of the wall.

4. The story doesn't tell us how wide the wall is, but there is some information that can help us guess. Which of the pieces of evidence below could help us imagine the Wall's width? (Choose one.)

   a. Part of the Wall was constructed of earth and wood.
   b. The road on top of the Wall allows five horses to walk side by side.
   c. The Wall is 3,700 miles long.

5. What evidence does the story contain that indicates there is little stone in the Gobi Desert?

   a. The towers are 40 feet high.
   b. In the desert, sand and pebbles covered with mud brick served as building materials.
   c. The Gobi is 1,500 miles from the Pacific.

ESCAPE FROM A UNION JAIL

The year was 1863. The North and South were fighting the Civil War. And Confederate General John Hunt Morgan was moving north with 2,500 cavalrymen. He and his men had carried out a series of destructive raids in Kentucky. Kentucky was part of Northern territory, and Confederate leaders hoped to disrupt the flow of Northern troops and equipment to the front.

In two years, General Morgan had risen from scout to general because of his brilliant military strategies. His successes, however, made him overconfident. Against orders from his superiors, he led his troops from Kentucky into Ohio. There, he and several of his men were captured. On July 31 Gen. Morgan and 69 of his cavalrymen were imprisoned in the Ohio State Penitentiary at Cincinnati.

Ohio State Penitentiary was a strong, well guarded, dog-patrolled prison. It was thought to be practically escape proof. But a short time after Morgan was placed in his prison cell, he noticed that the dirt floor was dry and free of mold. He concluded that there must be an air chamber or tunnel of some kind directly beneath the cellblock.

Morgan and his cellmates began digging beneath the floor. There were seven officers involved. Some dug with table knives. Others scooped up dirt with large Bowie knives. The dirt was hidden in mattresses from which the straw had been removed and burned. Finally, the men reached the walls of the hidden tunnel. They broke through nine inches of cement and several thicknesses of brick to gain entry to the tunnel itself. It proved to be six feet wide and four feet high, and it ran the entire length of the cell-block.

On November 26, after 23 days of work, the prisoners reached the area outside the prison building. But they were still inside the high walls which surrounded the prison grounds. From their tunnel hideout they cut through a five-foot inner wall, 12 feet of clay, and a six-foot outer wall. On the stormy night of November 27, they quietly emerged from beneath the outer wall. They cut the rope of the prison bell to keep guards from sounding the alarm, and faded into the darkness.

Gen. Morgan and his fellow officers eventually reached Confederate lines. He was given a new army command in Virginia. A year later he was killed in battle by Northern troops.

QUESTIONS

In the second paragraph we can find a good deal of information about Gen. Morgan.

1. What evidence seems to support the notion that he was ambitious and clever?

   a. He was overconfident.
   b. He was soon captured.
   c. He was placed in the Ohio State Penitentiary.
   d. He rose from scout to general in two years.

2. What evidence in the second paragraph indicates that Gen. Morgan was not the top ranking general in the Confederate Army?

   a. He was promoted from scout to general.
   b. He was captured.
   c. He went against the orders of his superiors.
   d. He was overconfident.

In the third and fourth paragraphs we are given a good deal of information regarding Morgan and his men while they were in prison.

3. What evidence is there that Morgan was a very careful observer?

   a. The prison was considered escape proof.
   b. The prison had a dog patrol.
   c. The men dug with table knives.
   d. Morgan noticed that the dirt floor was free of mold and moisture.

4. What evidence is there that Morgan and his men were not kept under constant observation? (Choose two.)

   a. They had Bowie knives.
   b. They were able to burn the straw from the mattresses.
   c. The tunnel ran the length of the cellblock.
   d. There were seven officers involved.

5. What evidence is there that Morgan and his men had a strong desire to escape? (Choose two.)

   a. They dug through all kinds of materials for a long time to get out.
   b. They spent very little time in the prison cell before they started digging.
   c. They scooped up dirt.
   d. They filled mattresses with dirt.

In the last two paragraphs we learn about their escape.

6. What evidence is there that Morgan was not unhappy with the Confederate Army?

   a. He and his men escaped on a stormy night.
   b. He took a new command in Virginia.
   c. The men cut the rope to the prison bell.

7. Drawing Conclusions

We draw conclusions about people and events every day. Sometimes we decide that we don't like something. That is a conclusion. Sometimes we decide that we have made a mistake. That is also a conclusion. A conclusion is a decision, an opinion, or an idea we come to after looking at a situation and thinking about the evidence.

Occasionally, we jump to conclusions too quickly. Then we must go back, examine the facts again, and change our conclusions. Poor conclusions often occur when we fail to examine all the facts in a situation.

Imagine that your neighbor is collecting animals for a business. You see him bring home a pig and a donkey. You know that he can use the hides of these animals to make leather. You conclude that he is starting a tanning factory. The next day he brings home two geese. You then conclude that he is starting a farm. He can't tan the hides of geese. On the third day he brings home an ostrich. At this point you conclude that he is probably starting a zoo. A regular farm probably wouldn't have an ostrich.

Notice that each of the facts in a situation must fit the conclusion. Learning to draw conclusions from what we read is an important critical thinking skill.

If, for example, you read a report that pointed out that the bald eagle is listed as an endangered animal in 43 states, you might conclude that
  a. The bald eagle is considered worth protecting.
  b. The bald eagle is in danger of dying out.
  c. People throughout the country have noticed the danger to the bald eagle.
  d. The bald eagle is living or has lived in many parts of the United States.

All of these conclusions are logically related to the fact that the bald eagle is listed on the endangered animal list in 43 states.

The report may also explain that there are many reasons for the deaths of the bald eagles. They die from poisons. They die from being shot by hunters. In addition, they die because the forests where they live have been cut down. Now you can conclude that
  a. People have been investigating the causes of the deaths.
  b. Correcting the problem will probably not be easy.

Finally, the report may explain that a team of scientists from New York state captured 118 baby eagles in Alaska. These babies were fed and cared for in New York state until they were old enough to hunt food on their own. Now you may conclude that
  a. Efforts are being made to replace dying eagles.
  b. Eagles have not died out in Alaska.
  c. It is possible to capture and transport eagles without seriously injuring them.

It is logical to conclude that scientists wouldn't hunt eagles where they had died out. It is also logical to conclude that the scientists would not transport so many eagles if the travel caused them to die.

See if you can decide which conclusions are justified after you read the story below.

Many sailors have died of thirst while they were surrounded by thousands of miles of ocean. They could not drink sea water for two reasons. First, there is often a huge number of germs in sea water. Second, the amount of salt in sea water is too great for the human body. This excessive amount of salt (about a quarter-pound of salt to a gallon of water) can lead to sickness and death.

1. Which conclusions would a careful reader make after reading the paragraph about sea water? (Choose one or more.)

   a. Sea water is bad for all kinds of living things.
   b. The waves in the ocean make the water bad for us.
   c. Supplies of fresh water are very important to people who are sailing across the ocean.
   d. You shouldn't use salt on your food for several months before you sail so your body will need and welcome lots of salt when you drink sea water.
   e. Sea water is not bad for you if you get used to it.

Answer: c

THE TALKING MACHINE

"Hi!" says the machine. "I'm the talking Coca-Cola vending machine. Make your selection, please." You push a button. The voice then says, "Thank you for using the talking vendor. Come again. Don't forget your change."

If you don't put in enough money, the machine says, "You need to deposit more money." If no more Coke is available, the machine says, "Sorry, sold out."

Most customers like the new talking machines. However, some people are annoyed by them. Generally, people tend to bring their friends back to see their new friend. This increases sales. In one location 100 cases of Coke were normally sold in a month. When the talking machine was installed there, 285 cases were sold in two weeks.

The novelty of the machine tends to wear off eventually. Yet there are always children who are interested. Machines in busy areas must be filled four times a day. There are usually little children around hoping to see the person inside who does the talking.

Sales have usually increased 30% with the talking machines. Overall, 85% of customers like these mechanical wonders. Some people buy the pop just to hear the machine. They may not want the drink itself. Some of the talking vendors speak in three languages — English, Spanish, and Japanese.

People who don't see the sign, "Try me, I can talk," often jump back when they hear the machine's voice for the first time.

QUESTIONS

1. In the story it says "the novelty of the machine wears off eventually." What conclusion can we draw from this information?

    a. The machine's sales in a particular location eventually decline.
    b. People now want talking machines in all busy areas.
    c. Adults are the only people buying Cokes.
    d. The machines are being given louder voices.

2. The story tells us that talking vending machines can speak in three languages. What conclusion can we draw from this information?

    a. The Coca-Cola company has decided to discontinue machines in this country.
    b. The Coca-Cola company wants to sell to people who speak other languages besides English.
    c. The Coca-Cola company thinks people will buy if they can't understand the directions.
    d. The Coca-Cola company wants to sell Coke only to people in Japan.

3. The story tells us that some people buy pop just to hear the machine talk. What conclusion can we draw from this information?

   a. Some people will learn to like Coke even though they don't like it now.
   b. Some of the Cokes that are bought may not be consumed.
   c. Some people didn't know it was a talking machine.
   d. Sales of Coke from machines are decreasing because people don't drink what they have bought.

PRESIDENTIAL ARRESTS

Only two United States Presidents have ever been arrested while in office. On a night in 1853, President Franklin Pierce was returning on horseback from the home of William Morgan in the southeastern part of Washington, D.C. In the pitch-black darkness, the President accidentally ran down Mrs. Nathan Lewis, who was crossing the street. A policeman, Stanley Edelin, arrested the chief executive for reckless horsemanship. According to police records, the President simply said, "I am Mr. Pierce," and he was released. The woman suffered little more than minor cuts and bruises.

Twice in 1866, Ulysses Grant, while still Commander of the Army of the Potomac, was arrested for speeding. In each case he was fined five dollars in precinct court. While he was President, Grant was racing his buggy west on Madison Street between 11th and 12th Avenues in Washington. Constable William West stepped out into the road and grabbed the horse's bridle. The horse dragged him 50 feet before it stopped. Officer West, a Union veteran, recognized Grant and began to apologize. But the President said, "Officer, do your duty."

The horse and buggy were taken to police headquarters and briefly impounded — but no charges were pressed because of the confusion over whether or not a President can be arrested without first being impeached by Congress.

QUESTIONS

1. When President Pierce was arrested for reckless horsemanship, he identified himself and was released. With this information, you may conclude

   a. President Pierce didn't really run over the woman.
   b. The woman wasn't hurt badly enough for the police to jail Pierce.
   c. Pierce was released because of his presidential position.

2. Which of the conclusions below is most appropriate based on U. S. Grant's arrest record?

   a. Apparently, Grant enjoyed driving his carriage at a high rate of speed.
   b. Grant used his prestigious office to get out of scrapes with the law.
   c. Grant believed the President should be allowed to drive as he wishes.

3. What piece of evidence in the story would lead you to conclude that President Grant felt his office did not make him immune to civilian law?

_____

_____

4. The first paragraph of the story probably leads you to conclude that

    a. Pierce intended to hit the woman in the street.
    b. Pierce did not protest when he was released because of his name.
    c. The injured woman required extensive medical care.

5. Read each of the statements below. If a statement is a valid conclusion based on the information in the story, put a check mark before it. If the statement is not a valid conclusion, leave it blank.

    a. At least on occasion, Grant drove his own carriage.
    b. Franklin Pierce was not tremendously concerned about the welfare of the woman he hit.
    c. No official records were made of these arrests.
    d. Both Presidents were probably guilty of a great many serious crimes.
    e. Grant wanted the police to treat him as any other citizen who had gone against the law.

6. The last paragraph of the story leads you to a conclusion about the relationship between a President and the law. Which of the following best describes that conclusion?

    a. At that time, a President was clearly under the same laws as any other citizen.
    b. At that time, the relationship between the President and the law was not clearly defined.
    c. At that time, a President was immune from arrest and punishment.

ANIMAL PSI

In August of 1923, Bobbie, a two-year-old Collie-English sheepdog, began his journey. He had become separated from his Oregon owners in a small Indiana town. After a period of uncertainty, he started his journey west. He went through Illinois and Iowa, sometimes catching rabbits and squirrels to survive and sometimes getting food from kindly people. He spent Thanksgiving and some weeks following the holiday with a family in Des Moines.

The journey was then resumed. He swam the ice-choked Missouri River, then crossed the icy slopes of the Rockies. The pads on his paws became so worn that the bones showed through the skin. In February, nearly six months after he began his amazing trip, he arrived at a farmhouse near Silverton, Oregon, where he had lived as a puppy. The next morning he strolled over to the restaurant of his owner and found his way up the stairs to the sleeping quarters. There his owner was sleeping after working a night shift in the restaurant.

How do we know where Bobbie went? The president of the Oregon humane society was able to reconstruct the journey after talking with people who had befriended Bobbie. The dog became one of history's canine heroes. He won medals, keys to cities, and even a gold collar.

How did he find his way home? He did not follow his master's route, and many people think that the dog found his way through a special sense or a type of ESP (extrasensory perception). Studies of animal behavior support the belief that there is an extra sense, or *animal psi (anpsi,* for short). *Anpsi* refers to an unexplained communication between an animal and its environment, or between an animal and a person or another animal, that occurs through undetected channels. Perhaps it was this special sense that led Bobbie all the way home.

QUESTIONS

1. Based on the information presented in the first paragraph, we can conclude that

   a. Bobbie's owners abandoned him in the Indiana town because they didn't want him.
   b. Bobbie sometimes got help from different people along the way.
   c. Bobbie immediately knew which way to travel when he was lost.

2. Reread Paragraph 2. Which two conclusions below are **not** supported by the information given in the paragraph?

   a. Bobbie didn't suffer at all from his long journey.
   b. Bobbie traveled several months to reach his owners.
   c. His owner was excited to see Bobbie.
   d. During his journey, Bobbie had to cross mountains and rivers.
   e. Bobbie's owner worked in a restaurant.

3. Based on the information in the story, which of the following is a valid conclusion?

   a. Bobbie's Oregon owner abused him when he was a puppy.
   b. Bobbie found his way home by using a special sense.
   c. Anpsi was the organization that helped trace Bobbie's journey.

4. The final paragraph leads us to conclude that

   a. There may be unexplained communication between people and animals.
   b. There is no evidence to support the idea of animal psi.
   c. An animal has no way of knowing what is happening in his environment.

5. Many people believe that Bobbie used *anpsi* to find his owner. What piece of evidence cited in the story could support this conclusion?

   a. Bobbie won medals, keys to cities, and a gold collar.
   b. His paws became worn from the journey.
   c. He did not follow his owner's route of travel to Oregon.

8. Predicting Outcomes

If we know that the very best ball team in a league is playing the very worst team, we can often guess who will win even before the game is played. The winning and losing records of the teams lead us to expect a victory for the team with the outstanding season. In a similar way, we can often predict what friends will choose or do if we know their strong likes and dislikes. Their choices are guided by their preferences — the desires they have shown in the past. Our predictions in both situations are based on the fact that events often continue in the same pattern or same direction that they followed earlier.

Sometimes, on the other hand, we can make predictions when something in a situation changes. We know that people react to change. Read the situations below. What do you think the people in each situation will do? Check your answers.

1. Robert Johnson is a wheat farmer. He has recently learned that a foreign nation plans to buy a great deal of wheat in the coming year. The price of wheat will go up rapidly. Farmer Johnson will probably

   a. not plant any wheat during the coming season
   b. plant a greater amount of wheat during the coming season
   c. plant corn instead of wheat during the coming year
   d. plant wheat but not fertilize it

2. The Public Library in Rivertown has had a great many books stolen in recent years, and it is very costly to replace them. Some citizens are afraid that the library will have to close. Miss Thomas, the librarian, is likely to

   a. close the library for good
   b. open the library on Sundays only
   c. check visitors carefully to see that they check books out
   d. borrow books from a library in a nearby town

As we read about characters in stories, we gradually learn whether they are bold or timid, selfish or generous, clever or foolish. On the basis of what we have learned about them, we can often predict their actions or guess at the results of their actions.

Try it yourself. Being able to make predictions about what will happen next in a story is an important reading and thinking skill. It helps you understand the direction that the story is going in, and what is happening to the characters in it. Read the two brief stories below, and indicate your predictions.

> Benjamin Banneker was a black scientist who lived at the time our country was being established. He was one of a few people who were chosen to draw up plans for a new city. The city was to be called Washington, D. C. The team of planners was led by a French engineer named L'Enfant.

> George Washington had a disagreement with L'Enfant, and the Frenchman went back to his country. He took the plans for Washington, D. C. with him. No one knew what to do.

Benjamin Banneker said that he had studied the plans and could draw them from memory. At first, the group of planners was skeptical. They could not believe that a person could remember so many thousands of details. Yet in a few months, Banneker reproduced the entire plan from memory. Banneker instructed the artists where to put each and every detail!

3. How did the members of the planning team probably view Banneker after this event?

   a. They lost faith in his ability to plan.
   b. The relied more upon his knowledge and skill.
   c. They decided to work without Banneker on the next project.
   d. They came to realize that Banneker was just lucky.

4. How did Banneker's career as a city planner probably change as a result of his work on the Washington project?

   a. He changed to another profession.
   b. He probably had more people interested in his services.
   c. He became better known throughout the country.
   d. He lost confidence in himself.
   e. He took very little pride in the capital city.

Josefina Guerrera saved many American lives during World War II. She was given the Medal of Freedom for her brave deeds.

Mrs. Guerrera lived in Manila, the capital city of the Philippines, at the time it was overrun by the Japanese Army. When the American troops left the Philippines, she asked to work for them as a spy. She promised them that she could get secret information from behind Japanese lines. She kept her promise.

Mrs. Guerrera began work immediately. She located Japanese fortifications. She found antiaircraft sites, and she sketched the locations of troop concentrations on large maps of the Philippines. Using her drawings, American pilots were able to pinpoint targets for bombing runs.

After American troops landed again in the Philippines, Mrs. Guerrera often spent weeks behind enemy lines. She always moved about in the open. For three years she scouted the territory held by the Japanese. One fact made her work particularly amazing. She was never searched and never caught by the Japanese. No enemy soldiers bothered her because she had the much-feared disease known as leprosy.

5. How do you think Japanese soldiers reacted to Mrs. Guerrera?

   a. The didn't want to have any contact with her.
   b. They decided that a person from Manila could not be a spy.
   c. They guessed that she was on their side because the Philippine people welcomed the Japanese invaders.

Answers: 1. b, 2. c, 3. b, 4. b and c, 5. a.

FAMILY CHAMPIONS

In Swanton, Vermont, near the Canadian border, you can find two arm-wrestling champions. Gilbert Trembloy of Swanton is ranked second in this country and fourth in the world in the 195-pound class. And his 13-year-old daughter, Kari, is the world's youngest champion in the 110-pound class.

Gil has arms that resemble tree trunks, and his shoulders are like small mountains. Kari is slim and shyly self-conscious. She has competed for only two years in arm-wrestling.

Trembloy has a car dealership. At the rear of his establishment, there are two rooms full of barbells and irons, plus two different styles of arm-wrestling tables. He works out three times a week and whenever business gets slow. Kari doesn't practice much, but occasionally she arm wrestles with her dad.

In her room, Kari has 16 trophies next to her bed. The biggest one is the world championship trophy she won in Brazil. Some of the contests are held in bars where minors are excluded. She is allowed in because people want to see her perform. About the world championship she says, "I was surprised." On one wall she has a collection of T-shirts emblazoned with bulging biceps, but she is not interested in acquiring huge arms herself.

QUESTIONS

1. Kari Trembloy probably became interested in arm wrestling because

   a. she thought more girls should participate in the sport
   b. her father is an arm-wrestling champion
   c. she wanted to prove that kids her age can be athletic champions

2. The story tells us that Gilbert Trembloy has arms that resemble tree trunks. This is probably because

   a. he works out three times a week
   b. he sometimes wrestles with his daughter
   c. he works in a car dealership

3. People probably want to see Kari in competition because

   a. they hope to see her famous father
   b. she is the world's youngest champion
   c. she competes in the same weight class as her father

4. The story does not tell us the number of contests Kari has competed in. How many has she most likely competed in?

   a. less than five
   b. no more than ten
   c. at least 16

5. Kari is an unusual arm-wrestling champion. Which of the answers below are probable reasons for her uniqueness?

  a. She lives near the Canadian border.
  b. She is 13 years old.
  c. She has a collection of T-shirts displaying bulging biceps.
  d. She is a girl.
  e. Her father owns a car dealership.
  f. She has won trophies.

6. If she continues to arm wrestle as she gets older, Kari will most likely

  a. move up to a higher weight class
  b. move to a big city
  c. not be allowed to compete in matches held in bars

MAROONED

In the early fall of 1809 Daniel Foss set sail for the Tonga Islands by way of the Cape of Good Hope. On March 25, Foss's ship, the *Negociator,* hit a submerged iceberg. Foss and 20 of his shipmates climbed into an open boat with a few provisions.

Within nine days, the 21-man crew had shrunk to eight. By January 10, only Foss and two others were still alive. One of the two died before land was sighted. Then the boat turned over in the breakers. Foss reached the shore of an island; his companion did not.

Foss explored the half-mile by quarter-mile island and found nothing except a few shellfish. He slept off and on for several days and was then awakened by a roar which turned out to be a herd of seals. He used the oar he had saved from the lifeboat as a club to get some food. Next he proceeded to dig holes in the island to get fresh water.

Eventually, Foss erected a stone hut and, on the highest point on the island, a 30-foot tower. At the top of this tower, he attached his tattered shirt. He used his oar for many things. He carved out the story of his stay on it. He wrote at the rate of 12 letters of the alphabet per day.

In his sixth year on the island he saw a ship. A small landing boat had put out from the ship and was trying to get to the rocky coast. Foss, hanging on to his precious oar, dived into the surf. He got to the ship and eventually to his home in Elkton, Maryland. His oar was presented to the Peale Museum in Philadelphia, but the museum no longer exists, and the oar has disappeared.

QUESTIONS

1. After the *Negociator* hit the iceberg, it is likely that it eventually

  a. drifted for several hundred miles
  b. sank
  c. was repaired by another ship's crew

2. The story doesn't tell us why the other crewmen in the open boat died. Which of the following are probably reasons for their deaths?

    a. lack of food and fresh water
    b. the hard work of rowing
    c. mutiny and murder

3. When his boat turned over, Foss swam to an island. His companion most likely

    a. stayed with the boat until another ship rescued him
    b. reached the other side of the island
    c. drowned

4. Foss survived on the island probably because of

    a. his clever use of the few things he had with him
    b. the size of the island
    c. the food and supplies that washed ashore from the lifeboat

5. The island Foss lived on was probably

    a. populated by tribes of natives
    b. a port for many ships
    c. uninhabited

6. When Foss finally returned to his Maryland home, people probably

    a. greeted him like a hero
    b. rejected him because he had been gone too long
    c. hated him because he didn't save any of his shipmates

WHEN TRAINS FIRST RAN UNDERGROUND

One day in the late 1800's Alfred Ely Beach looked out of his New York office window at the crowds on the streets below. He decided he needed to do something about the crowding. He was the editor of *Scientific American,* already at that time one of the great science magazines. He was also an inventor of proven talents. He had already invented a typewriter for the blind and a cable system.

Beach decided that some of the traffic from the streets would have to be moved either above the ground or below the ground. After thinking it over, he decided an above-ground system would be too noisy. He chose to build underground.

Neither the electric motor nor the gasoline engine had been invented. Steam engines powered by coal were widely used, but Beach was afraid that a steam engine would produce too much heat and soot in an underground tunnel. Finally, he decided that forced air was the best answer.

The big challenge for Beach was not building the project, but getting permission to do so. New York officials at the time were very crooked. They expected to receive bribes, but Beach would not pay blackmail. Therefore, he decided to build in secret.

First, Beach got a permit to construct a small model train below Broadway, using forced air. But instead of building the smaller train, Beach instructed his men to dig a tunnel nine feet in diameter and 312 feet long. The work was completed in 58 nights. City officials didn't find out about it until it was done. The train car that was built to run in the tunnel carried 20 passengers. It was moved along the tracks by a giant fan which, in turn, was powered by a steam engine on the surface of the ground. When the direction of the fan blade was reversed, the train was pushed backwards.

To make the station attractive, Beach added a waiting room with paintings, a grand piano, and a large goldfish tank. The opening of the line was a smashing success.

In the end, crooked city officials stopped the plan. The project was abandoned and even forgotten until 1912. At that time a crew digging a new subway cut through the wall of Beach's tunnel. They were astonished to find the elegant station and Beach's train still standing on the tracks.

QUESTIONS

It is interesting to consider how things might have been different had Alfred Beach been very close to city officials.

1. What would probably have happened if Alfred Beach had gotten permission to build the full-sized subway?

    a. He would have powered it differently.
    b. He would have given up his editorship of the *Scientific American*.
    c. He would have ended up in jail.
    d. He would have extended the subway to serve other parts of the city.

2. When Alfred Beach was blocked by city officials from continuing his underground subway, it is likely that (Choose 2.)

    a. he started building the transportation system above ground
    b. he had difficulty getting people to invest money in his project
    c. he turned his talents to other projects
    d. he wrecked the subway so that others couldn't use it

3. The reason Beach had the men dig at night was probably because

    a. the men hated to give up their day-time jobs
    b. the men needed the money
    c. Beach wanted to hide the project from city officials
    d. there was no time during the day to dig

4. When the 1912 subway project was underway, the diggers ran into Beach's station and subway tunnel. What do you think happened? (Choose two.)

a. Newspaper reporters gathered at the scene to report the finding.

b. The new project was abandoned so that the old tunnel would not be disturbed.

c. The new subway was continued even though it meant the destruction of the old tunnel.

d. The new subway planners switched to using fans to push the subway trains.

9. Facts, Probabilities, and Opinions

One of the most important of all critical thinking skills is the ability to distinguish among statements of fact, statements of opinion, and statements of probability.

Statements of fact can be proved or disproved. They are either true or false. A statement like "Roses are often red" is a statement of fact. So is "My sister is five feet nine inches tall." Even an untrue statement like "A kangaroo is a kind of bird" is a statement of fact. You can prove that it's not true.

Statements of opinion, on the other hand, tell us what someone likes or dislikes. They tell us what some people consider valuable or what they consider to be of little or no importance. A statement like "Binkies are the best tasting candy in the world" is a statement of opinion. So is "Luisa is fun to be with," or "Gene looks handsome in his new suit," or "Algebra is dumb."

Statements of probability are guesses or predictions about the future. "It will snow tomorrow" is a statement of probability. So is "Someday, Jeannine will be elected President of the United States." So is "If the army crosses the border, there will be war."

> **Facts** usually give specific information. (The plant is seven inches tall. It is dark green in color.) **Opinions** about the plant give people's reactions to it. (It is a very pretty plant. It has a lovely shape.) **Probabilities** refer to the future of the plant. (If it remains healthy, it will probably grow to be 45 inches tall.)

1. Can you tell the differences among statements of fact, statements of opinion, and statements of probability? Read the statements below and write "fact," "probability," or "opinion" beside each sentence.

   _____ a. Belgium is a great country.

   _____ b. Ken will be furious when he sees this.

   _____ c. Basketball is an exciting and colorful sport.

   _____ d. Dogs make better pets than cats.

   _____ e. The house Velma lives in is the prettiest one in town.

   _____ f. Everyone should work to help support themselves.

   _____ g. Terry is older than Betty.

   _____ h. Sue is going to college next year.

   _____ i. If everything goes well, we'll be home by five o'clock.

   _____ j. Ruth is certainly the cutest girl in the eighth grade.

   _____ k. It is five o'clock in Paris at this time.

   _____ l. It is going to be a long, hot summer.

   _____ m. Sunday is the third day of the month.

_____ n. Rahim is my cousin.

_____ o. Joy is the captain of the soccer team.

_____ p. Jane came to class late today.

_____ q. Alan lives in the fourth house on the left side of the street.

Sometimes we find both facts and probabilities in the same sentence. Look at the statement below.

John told the team that they will win.

Notice that it is a **fact** that John made the statement, yet the declaration he made is really a statement of **probability.**

2. See if you can pick out the **two** kinds of statements in each of the sentences below. There may be a factual statement and an opinion, there may be a factual statement followed by another factual statement, or there may be a factual statement and a statement of probability. Write "fact," "opinion," or "probability" in each of the blanks below the statements to give your answers.

a. Mary thought that ostriches run faster than horses.

_____   _____

b. Ralph won the prize, but he'll never compete again.

_____   _____

c. Tom misjudged the ball and struck out.

_____   _____

d. Sarah feels that wrestling is the best sport of all to watch.

_____   _____

LIVE MINIATURES

J. C. Williams of Inman, South Carolina, is one of the world's largest short-order animal breeders. He has short horses, goats, and sheep, and now a new breed — short zebu cattle. Fashion designers, foreign dignitaries, Arab sheiks, and celebrities from all over the world have been charmed by Williams' miniature animals, which sell for as much as $35,000 apiece.

The horses are the most popular. There is something very appealing about these tiny creatures, which are perfect in every detail — just like their grown-up cousins. They are not unlike the large stuffed ponies we see in toy stores, but *these* gentle miniatures can frolic about and respond to their owners in loving ways. Williams' horselets are about 17 inches tall when they're born, and they grow to a maximum of 34 inches. That's smaller than the smallest pony and only slightly taller than a large dog.

Williams' 120-acre Dell Tera Mini Horse Farm now has approximately 400 small horses and 200 other wee beasties. It all started about ten years ago when one mare produced a 12½-inch foal. The *National Enquirer* took pictures of the tiny foal, and Williams said, "From that day on, we've gotten mail by the pickup load."

Of the estimated 250 adult horses 30 inches or smaller in the United States, Williams has 50. The other miniature animals sell well, but Williams expects the zebu cattle, miniature versions of the hump-backed cattle of India, to be very popular in the coming years.

QUESTIONS

In each pair of statements below, write **F** next to the statement of fact and **O** next to the statement of opinion.

1. a. _____ Williams' miniature animal farm includes horses, sheep, and goats.
   b. _____ Williams is a clever businessman.

2. a. _____ The first miniature that Williams' farm produced was a foal.
   b. _____ The miniature horses are the best ones to buy.

3. a. _____ The animals are too small to be of any use to their owners.
   b. _____ The horses are about 17 inches tall at birth.

4. Based on the information in the story, which of the following probabilities is **most** likely to occur?

   a. Williams will eventually stop producing the miniature horses because they don't sell well.
   b. None of the animals mentioned in the story will be very popular in the future.
   c. The zebu cattle will increase in popularity in the next few years.

5. In Williams' opinion, which of the following animals will go up most in popularity in the future?

    a. the goats

    b. the zebu cattle

    c. the sheep

6. The statements below are made up of both fact and opinion. In each sentence, underline the part that is purely **factual.**

    a. Williams' first tiny animal appeared in the *National Enquirer,* a lousy magazine.

    b. Williams' small animals are really odd looking; he has about 600 of them.

    c. In 1981, Williams sold half a million dollars worth of the miniature animals, so he is a very smart man.

THE MAGNETIC ART OF MESMERISM

Did you know that there was once a doctor who tried to cure his patients by waving magnets at them? And even stranger, his cures worked! He was an Austrian physician named Anton Mesmer, and he is remembered today as the father of hypnotism.

Mesmer lived in the 1700's, and his discovery was accidental. In his day, scientists were doing the first basic experiments with electricity and magnets. Mesmer decided to find out what effects magnets had on people. In particular, he hoped to find a medical use for magnetism.

Mesmer discovered that he could cure a number of sick people by passing magnets over their bodies. Later he found that all that was really necessary to bring about a cure was to touch the person or have the subject drink a glass of "magnetized" water. Finally, he was able to bring about cures without using a magnet at all. But he was unwilling to give up his ideas about magnets. He decided that something he called "animal magnetism" was effecting the cures.

The doctors in Austria denounced Mesmer as a fraud and a quack. He moved to Paris and built a thriving practice. He organized group healing sessions over which he would preside, dressed in long, colorful robes. He would wave a wand over the heads of his believing subjects. These unorthodox treatments caused him to be denounced in France as well.

What Mesmer did not realize was that his cures were really based on what later came to be known as hypnotism. Some doctors use hypnotism today, but they still cannot agree on what happens inside the minds and bodies of their subjects. Some modern hypnotists "mesmerize" their patients and instruct their minds to make them better. This is what Mesmer had succeeded in doing, but hypnotism today is treated with more respect than it was in his time.

QUESTIONS

1. Mark the statements below with an **F** if they are statements of fact, with an **O** if they are statements of opinion, and with a **P** if they are statements of probability.

   a. _____ Anton Mesmer's cures were based on hypnotism.
   b. _____ In the future, hypnotism will be used more frequently with mental patients.
   c. _____ People who believe in hypnotism are crazy.
   d. _____ Mesmer's name will someday be treated with more respect than it was in his time.
   e. _____ Mesmer often conducted group curing sessions.

2. The sentences below contain both facts and opinions. In each sentence, underline the part that is purely **opinion.**

   a. Mesmer was an Austrian physician who was a quack.
   b. Some doctors use hypnotism today because they like to play magician.
   c. Mesmer waved wands over his subjects — what a stupid idea!

3. What were the opinions of the Austrian doctors about Mesmer's ideas?

   a. They approved of his practices with hypnotism.
   b. They thought he was a phony.
   c. They used many of his ideas with their own patients.

Add one statement of opinion to each of the two factual statements below to form mixed fact and opinion statements like the ones in Question 2 above.

4. Mesmer used magnets to cure patients . . . _____

   _____

5. Some doctors use hypnotism today . . . _____

   _____

6. Carefully read each of the factual statements below. Then cross out the number of words indicated in the parentheses to change each factual statement into a statement of opinion. The first one is done for you.

   a. ~~Some scientists think~~ hypnotism is a valuable medical tool. (Cross out three words.)
   b. Some doctors thought Mesmer was a quack. (Cross out three words.)
   c. Mesmer believed most people should be treated with magnets. (Cross out two words.)
   d. He is frequently remembered as a fraud. (Cross out three words.)

65

THE REAL MERMAIDS

Sailors, storytellers, and movie makers love to tell tales of beautiful mermaids who live in the depths of the ocean. Of course, mermaids don't actually exist. But there are two kinds of sea animals that strangely resemble the legendary mermaids. They are the manatees of the tropical Atlantic and their cousins the dugongs of the Indian Ocean.

Manatees and dugongs have bodies something like dolphins. But unlike dolphins, they often stand upright in the water, holding their flippers in front of them like arms. From a distance, they appear remarkably like humans. Close up, however, the resemblance ends. They have none of the mermaid's beauty. They have bald heads, fat wrinkled necks, a bristly mustache, and a face like a tuskless walrus. Nevertheless, many scientists think that these curious water animals could have given rise to the legends of mermaids and mermen.

Manatees are fairly common in the shallow rivers of Florida. One of the few people to study manatees, O. N. Barrett, says that these creatures are also fairly common in bayous, lagoons, and rivers along the coast of Nicaragua. Families consist of a bull, a cow, and a calf or two. They normally join a herd of 10 to 50 individual manatees living along a particular stretch of river during the day. They scatter at night to graze. The head is often held well above water, when they are chewing. Their armlike flippers poke grass toward their mouths. The noise made by their upper lips and crunching teeth can be heard for some distance. The sound resembles horses grazing in a pasture.

The manatee's cousin, the dugong, is a creature of coasts and the open sea. It seldom ventures into rivers as the manatee does. The dugong has almost never been caught alive. Few naturalists have seen it. Mrs. Barrett did, however, have a chance to view one when fishermen in Mozambique in Africa caught one of these curious creatures in a net. The unexpected catch caused a great deal of excitement. The dugong was eventually given to a blacksmith who embalmed it and took it to Johannesburg, South Africa. There he made a small fortune exhibiting the body as — of course — a mermaid, half fish and half human.

QUESTIONS

There are a number of statements about manatees and dugongs in the story. Several of the observations are **statements of fact.** We are told, for example, that these animals are common in certain regions, that they graze at night, and that they hold their bodies upright in the water while grazing. Some of the observations are **statements of opinion.** We are told, for example, that manatees and dugongs resemble the legendary mermaids. We could not prove this statement in the same way that we verify statements of fact. If the author told us that manatees will likely disappear before the year 2000, we would have a **statement of probability.**

Read the statements below and write "fact," "opinion," or "probability" in the blank beside each.

_____ **1.** Families consist of a bull, a cow, and a calf or two.

_____ **2.** Hunters will soon begin to shoot these animals.

_____ 3. Dugongs seldom venture into fresh water.

_____ 4. Dugongs are the ugliest animals on earth.

_____ 5. Manatees are not really worth having around.

_____ 6. The noise made by their upper lips and crunching teeth can be heard for some distance.

_____ 7. The dugong has a tail shaped like a dolphin's.

_____ 8. Mrs. Barrett had a chance to see a dugong.

_____ 9. Exhibiting the dugong as a mermaid was a cheap thing to do.

_____ 10. The blacksmith took the embalmed dugong to Johannesburg, South Africa.

_____ 11. The people who paid to see the embalmed dugong in South Africa were really stupid.

_____ 12. The manatees use their flippers to poke grass into their mouths when they feed.

_____ 13. Dugongs should be protected by law so they won't become an extinct species.

_____ 14. If people from New York City saw dugongs, they would be fooled just like the South Africans were tricked.

_____ 15. If we would leave the manatees alone, they would become less timid and would graze during daylight hours.

_____ 16. Fishermen from Mozambique caught a dugong in their fishing nets.

_____ 17. If Mother Nature didn't want manatees on earth, she wouldn't have put them here.

_____ 18. Manatees scatter at night.

_____ 19. It would be fun to have a manatee for a pet because people would be really curious about it.

10. Author's Purpose and Point of View

Authors write articles, stories, and books for a number of reasons. Sometimes they write to amuse or entertain us. Joke books, for example, add humor and laughter to our lives. Sometimes they seek to inform us. History books and biographies help introduce us to life in an earlier period of time. Still other writers attempt to change the way we think about important topics. It has been suggested, for example, that the story of *Uncle Tom's Cabin* about the mistreatment of slaves actually hastened the beginning of the American Civil War.

Whenever we read something, we should be aware of the author's purpose in writing it. Is it written to inform? To amuse? To give information? To convince us of something? We should also be aware of the author's point of view on what he or she is writing about. Is the author for it? Against it? Neutral?

When we are thinking critically about an author's purpose and point of view, we must be aware of the language he or she is using. Authors choose their words carefully to give the effect they want. For example, let's say a company and a labor union are trying to work out a wage agreement. A writer who is strongly on the company's side might write, "The union is trying once again to milk money out of the company." Another writer who is equally strongly on the side of the union might write, "The union is struggling to get a fair shake for all the employees." The facts are the same, but the writers' opinions are very different. And so the impressions you get of what's happening is very different, too.

Notice how we can slant the descriptions of people by the choice of words that describe them:

	If we like them we describe them as:	If we don't like them we describe them as:
Let's assume that we know someone who is **hard to convince** . . .	firm	stubborn
We may know someone who is **emotional** . . .	warmhearted	mushy
An acquaintance may be **daring** . . .	courageous	reckless
We may have a friend who is **cautious** . . .	careful	cowardly
We may know someone who **cares about others** . . .	thoughtful	do-gooder

1. See if you can pick out the ***more negative word*** in each of the statements below:

    a. Jim's behavior was obviously (brutal/unkind).
    b. The trip to the store was (unnecessary/useless).
    c. Sue had a very (clever/sneaky) way about her.
    d. Tom was certainly a (carefree/shiftless) person.
    e. Margaret was a (homely/plain) girl.
    f. Ted was (fat/chubby).
    g. Terry was usually (inactive/sluggish).

In addition to choosing loaded words, authors sometimes seek to influence their readers by carefully focusing on specific details in describing people and events. If an author is against professional boxing, for example, he or she may tell a great deal about the serious injuries and early deaths of fighters. If, on the other hand, the writer favors professional boxing, the focus may be on thrilling and sensational bouts in which champions fought with inspiring courage. It is up to the reader to recognize what is being left out or downplayed in a story or report.

Notice how the story below uses both carefully chosen details and loaded words to create sympathy for the girls of China who had their feet bound. Until 1900, the Chinese considered tiny feet to be an important mark of beauty among women. The most esteemed women and girls had "Golden Lotus" feet. These were no more than four or five inches long.

Most Chinese girls were seven years old when their feet were first bound. Their families would select a special day when the stars were in a favorable pattern. The parents would then wind a long cloth tightly around the toes and heels of each girl so that the toes and heels were pulled together. Walking with their feet bound like this caused unbearable pain. It was even difficult for the girls to sleep because their feet felt as though they were on fire. The feet swelled and sometimes they would bleed. Occasionally, one or two toes would drop off. If the girls loosened the wrappings, they would be severely punished.

The girls' feet didn't stop growing, of course. They simply became deformed to fit the bindings. The bindings were redone every two weeks, and the girls were fitted with a new pair of smaller shoes. Their families walked them around so that they would get used to walking on bound feet.

The pain lasted about a year. After two years of binding, the feet of the little girls became practically dead. This presented other problems. In the summer the deadened feet smelled terribly, and in the winter the poor blood circulation made them feel dreadfully cold. Regardless of the consequences, the feet had to be kept continually bound.

2. Notice the words and details that the author uses to make us feel sorry for the girls. The phrases "unbearable pain," "feet on fire," and "the feet swelled" are all mentioned. Try to list five other words or details that the author uses to create sympathy.

    a. _____

    b. _____

c. _____

d. _____

e. _____

COMMUNICATING WITH SPIRITS

Modern spiritualism, the belief that the living can communicate with the dead, began in a cottage in Hydesville, New York, on March 31, 1848. The occupants of that cottage were John and Mary Fox and their two youngest daughters, Margaret and Kate, about 11 and 15.

In March of 1848, three months after they moved into the house, the girls heard noises at night and asked to sleep in their parents' room. On March 31, Kate snapped her fingers in the dark. "Mr. Splitfoot, do as I do," she called out and clapped her hands. The clapping was echoed instantly. Then Maragaret gave a command with the same results.

Next, Mrs. Fox asked the spirit to rap out her children's ages. That was done quickly and correctly. Then Mrs. Fox asked, "Is that a human being?" No answer. "Is it a spirit? Rap twice if it is." Two sounds were heard. Further questions revealed that the rapper was the spirit of a man who had been murdered in the house. His body was later found during the moving of old partitions.

The Fox sisters became famous. They gave public demonstrations throughout the country. The reaction of the public was astonishing; it was as if a great dam gave way. Virtually overnight spiritualism exploded into a full-blown movement. Mediums by the hundreds began to demonstrate their powers.

The spiritualism movement in its heyday lasted for 50 years. It hasn't entirely died out yet. Such things as national tragedies where many people are killed will often trigger revivals of spiritualism both here and in other countries.

QUESTIONS

In each pair of statements below, decide which one shows a negative attitude on the part of the writer.

1. a. Spiritualism is the belief that the living can communicate with the dead.
   b. Spiritualism is the silly idea that the living and the dead can communicate.

2. a. The Fox sisters became notorious.
   b. The Fox sisters became famous.

3. a. Mediums began to show off their tricks.
   b. Mediums began to demonstrate their powers.

4. The author probably wrote this article because

   a. he wanted people to learn how to talk to spirits
   b. he wanted to provide information about the beginnings of spiritualism
   c. he wanted to make the government outlaw public demonstrataions of spiritualism

5. What may the author mean when he states that spiritualism hasn't entirely died out *yet*?

    a. Spiritualism will never die out.
    b. Interest in spiritualism may eventually decline.
    c. A belief in spiritualism has not been seen in many years.

6. Do you think the author believes in spiritualism?

    a. definitely yes
    b. definitely no
    c. difficult to tell from the article

CAN FINGERS SEE?

Early in 1963, a young woman was being tested by Soviet scientists. They had heard about the young lady who could "see" with her fingertips. As any scientist knows, this is utter nonsense. But Roza Kuleshova gladly performed for them. She explained that she had discovered this unusual talent when she was 16 years old, after both of her eyes were heavily bandaged following an accident in her home.

The scientists covered her eyes with adhesive tape and foil, and even had her wear a large metal diving helmet. Without hesitation she read page after page in books and magazines through her fingertips. She described photographs in publications she had never seen before. She even described colors in pictures!

To "see" with her fingertips, the young woman moved them along the page about half an inch above the part she was examining. She could also read and describe colors by putting her fingers on or well above the pages. But she found it was easier when she didn't touch the material. Roza was able to describe scenes and people in great detail in glossy photos. The Soviet Academy of Sciences agreed that she did indeed "see" with her fingertips, but they did not know how she did it.

The talent is rare but not unprecedented. In 1898, Dr. Khorrin of the Neuro-Psychiatric Hospital in Tambov tested a similar subject and published his findings. During the 1920's, Dr. Jules Romain of Paris tested more than a score of blind people who could "see" through their skins. In Elkton, Virginia, Margaret Foos also baffled scientists in 1961 with her ability to see without the use of her eyes.

QUESTIONS

1. Look at the groups of words below. In each group, circle the word that has a more negative tone than the others.

    a. ability trick talent
    b. nonsense doubtful unlikely
    c. tested examined grilled
    d. baffled tricked confused

2. The author believes that Roza Kuleshova

   a. lied about her ability to see with her fingers
   b. proved to the skeptical scientists that she had an unusual ability to describe printed material by using her fingers
   c. was crazy because she thought she could see with her hands

3. What may the author mean by putting the word **see** in quotation marks?

   a. The young lady only thought she could read books through her fingertips.
   b. She couldn't actually see things with her fingers in the same manner she could see them with her eyes.
   c. She used some kind of trick to fool the scientists into thinking she could see with her fingers.

4. Circle the three words below that best explain how the author feels about the reported cases of people who can see without the use of their eyes.

confused	fascinated	intrigued
skeptical	unsure	indifferent
convinced	doubtful	bored

5. What seems to be the author's opinion about an ability to see through the fingertips?

   a. The author thinks the ability is complete foolishness.
   b. The author can find no evidence to support the idea of fingertip sight.
   c. The author feels that some people do, indeed, possess this unusual talent.

ACROSS THE ATLANTIC IN A TINY SAILBOAT

In 1978 Gerry Spies finished building his tiny sailboat in his garage. He named her *Yankee Girl*. He took the ten-foot boat out on White Bear Lake in Minnesota for some final testing. By July 1, 1979, the boat had been transported to the East coast. Soon he had her rigged and he was on his way to England.

Yankee Girl was equipped with both sails and a motor. The motor helped move the tiny ship out of the harbor into the open sea. Then the sails took over. The first five days were rough. Gerry could eat only fruit, dried beef, crackers, and a peanut butter sandwich because the boat rocked so much it made his stomach queasy. On the sixth day, when gentle winds made the tiny boat more stable, everything seemed brighter. Gerry could then enjoy his hot beef stew.

During the first eight days at sea, the sun was in view only three times. The winds, however, were general calm. In fact, there were only 12 hours of favorable winds. On the ninth day, Gerry reached the Gulf Stream. The next morning he sighted a ship. He was able to talk to people on board the ship and get a message home to his wife, Sally.

During the next four days, the weather grew worse and finally erupted into violence. A 17-foot wave caught Gerry with his hatch cover open. He managed to get back into the hold, but he could not fasten the cover. Water poured in, and he began bailing furiously. The bailing was so tiring that it seemed to him like he was trying to empty the whole ocean with a spoon.

The storm finally subsided, but not before Gerry had been soaked for many hours. When he tried to change his clothes, he removed the top layer of skin as well. On the 15th day he had another terrifying dunking. This time he was thrown into the sea. Luck was with him, however. A second wave righted the small boat and flung him back on deck.

Finally, the worst of Gerry's problems were over. On July 24 he docked at Falmouth, England. There was a huge celebration. Gerry had succeeded in crossing the Atlantic in the smallest boat in the history of ocean crossings.

Gerry's Atlantic crossing, however, did not completely satisfy his urge to sail. On June 1, 1981, he and *Yankee Girl* left for Sydney, Australia. They arrived safely in Sydney harbor on October 31, 1981.

QUESTIONS

1. The author who wrote this story obviously wanted to stress some aspects of the trip over other considerations. Which of the following aspects of the trip did this author stress?

   a. The technical construction of the ship.
   b. The scenery that could be seen on the trip.
   c. The cooperation among people in making the trip possible.
   d. The difficult challenges a man faces in crossing the Atlantic Ocean in a tiny boat.

2. The author of the story has chosen to present Gerry in a certain way. What kind of feeling do you get regarding the kind of person Gerry is?

   a. He likes to get away from his family.
   b. He enjoys the challenge and the struggle of such a trip.
   c. He made the trip to get personal attention.
   d. He likes painful experiences because he feels guilty.

3. The author can highlight any part of the whole trip that he wants to explain in detail. What aspect of the trip did he tell about in most detail?

   a. The celebration Gerry had upon reaching Falmouth.
   b. The attitudes of Gerry's family and friends concerning the trip.
   c. The religious feelings one gets when one is alone in a threatening situation.
   d. The specific problems one faces in a small boat during storms.

4. The author could have ended the story with the celebration at Falmouth. What is a good reason for adding the information about the trip to Sydney?

   a. The author can show that people from other parts of the world would also welcome Gerry.
   b. The author can emphasize that Gerry considered the trip a good experience and wanted to set new records.
   c. The author can show that Gerry's wife is very understanding regarding his absence from home.
   d. The author can show that people can get "hooked" on travel to a point where they throw away their lives on crazy stunts.

5. What aspect of a storm at sea does the author choose to emphasize most?

   a. beauty
   b. unpredictability
   c. scientific interest
   d. violence

6. What do you think the author feels about Gerry?

   a. admires him
   b. envies him
   c. distrusts him
   d. is indifferent to him

D. Putting It All Together

The second section of this book contains ten stories, with several questions after each story. The questions test you on your ability to handle all the skills taught in this book. Next to each one is a box that lists the skill you need to answer the question. If you wish, you can go back to the chapter in which the skill was taught for a quick review.

1. Hurricane Camille

To live through a really big hurricane is to experience terror that leaves you speechless and shaken. It is an unreal nightmare of violence and fear. Hurricane Camille, which visited our southern coast on August 17, 1969, was just such a hurricane.

As a result of the relentless pounding and fury of the winds, 19,467 homes and 700 businesses were destroyed and 241 people were killed. Hurricane warnings had been broadcast, and 150,000 people heeded them. But others thought they could ride out the storm. They didn't know what they were in for. In the darkness, rain and terrifying winds pounded homes and battered down walls. The electricity went off, and houses tumbled from their foundations and were smashed to pieces. Cargo ships snapped from their moorings.

Seawater 25 to 30 feet deep poured in upon the unfortunate residents. In Gulfport, Mississippi, a 900,000 gallon oil tank was hurled 3½ miles from its original site. Telephone poles snapped like toothpicks. The roar was deafening as winds quickly gusted to 200 miles per hour. Everything in a 70-mile-wide path was devastated.

On August 18, residents returned to an unbelievable pile of wreckage dotted with human and animal bodies. The federal government sent in over 200 tons of food and hundreds of mobile homes and classrooms. The cleanup took many months and a prodigious amount of hard work. Even though the storm was over, no one who lived through it would ever forget the force of Hurricane Camille.

QUESTIONS

| PREDICTING OUTCOMES |

1. The story tells us that 150,000 people heeded the warnings about the hurricane. It is likely that these people

   a. stayed in their homes
   b. left their homes for safer locations
   c. waited until the National Guard came to help them

| MAIN IDEA |

2. Which of the possible story titles below would be the most suitable alternate title for this story?

   a. "A Slight Storm"
   b. "Federal Government Aid"
   c. "A Violent Storm's Fury"

| CITING EVIDENCE |

3. Which of the following pieces of evidence was used in the selection to support the statement, "A hurricane is an unreal nightmare of violence and fear."

   a. During the storm, houses were smashed.
   b. 241 people died in the storm.
   c. Oil tankers load and unload at Gulfport, Mississippi.
   d. Telephone poles snapped in two because of the strong winds.
   e. Electrical power will sometimes go off for a short time during a storm.

CONTEXT AND WORD MEANINGS

4. "The cleanup after Hurricane Camille took many long months and a ***prodigious*** amount of hard work." In this sentence, the italicized word means

    a. huge

    b. short

    c. modest

ADEQUACY OF INFORMATION

5. Which of the following pieces of information is ***not*** included in the story?

    a. During the storm, cargo ships were forced from their moorings.

    b. Television news programs spent several days covering the aftermath of Hurricane Camille.

    c. The storm winds gusted up to 200 miles per hour.

AUTHOR'S POINT OF VIEW

6. The author wants us to think that

    a. people are foolish to be frightened of hurricanes

    b. a hurricane is one of the most violent storms in nature

    c. people who are fortunate enough to experience a hurricane are lucky

2. The Ancient Roots of Kung Fu

Ancient Shaolin Monastery at the foot of Song Mountain in China seems like just another of the many old monasteries founded to teach the Buddhist religion. But Shaolin is special. For here, in an earlier time, Shaolin's soldier-monks invented the martial art of kung fu.

Shaolin Monastery did not begin as a center for warlike activities. It was a place for meditation and prayer. According to tradition, an Indian monk named Bodhidharma settled in the area in about 525 A. D. His mission was to teach the form of Buddhism called Zen.

From the discipline of Zen meditation sprang a deadly form of combat. This combat is a fast and acrobatic style of self-defense made popular in the United States by Bruce Lee in the movies and in the television series "Kung Fu." When it was in its heyday, Shaolin Monastery had 2,000 soldier-monks who wielded long sticks and bare fists to defend themselves against bandits and Japanese pirates.

When the Communists came to power in China in the 1940's, they tried to suppress Buddhism. The monastery was damaged in three fires during the 1960's and 1970's. It was then closed by the government. Shi Dauchan, the last true Shaolin master, was jailed. But now, Shaolin is once again revered by the Chinese. Some of China's young men are once again being taught kung fu. Peking plans to have a movie made by Hong Kong filmmakers depicting the swashbuckling Shaolin soldier-monks. It is all part of modern China's attempt to recapture some of its historical heritage.

QUESTIONS

| MAIN IDEA | **1.** This story is mainly about |

      a. the history of Shaolin Monastery and kung fu
      b. the history of Buddhism
      c. the history of Zen meditation

| CONTEXT AND WORD MEANINGS | **2.** "Modern interest in kung fu is part of China's attempt to *recapture* its historical heritage." In this sentence, the underlined word means |

      a. discover
      b. get back
      c. get rid of

CITING
EVIDENCE

3. Which three of the following statements are evidence of modern interest in the art of kung fu?

    a. "Kung Fu" was a popular television show.
    b. Shi Dauchan was the last true Shaolin master.
    c. Peking officials are producing a movie about the Shaolin soldier-monks.
    d. The monastery was damaged by fires.
    e. Bruce Lee's movies were very popular in the 1970's.

PREDICTING
OUTCOMES

4. Based on the information in the last paragraph, kung fu will probably

    a. die out in China
    b. become increasingly popular in China
    c. become illegal in China

SEQUENCE

5. Number the following events from 1 to 3 according to the sequence in which they took place. (Use *1* for the first event and *3* for the last.)

    __ Fires damaged the monastery.
    __ Shaolin monks developed kung fu.
    __ Bodhidharma taught Zen Buddhism.

AUTHOR'S
POINT OF
VIEW

6. The author of this story wants us to think that

    a. kung fu is savage and cruel
    b. kung fu is skillful and exciting
    c. kung fu is silly and boring

3. The Elegant Rolls-Royce

A Rolls-Royce is both a symbol of luxury and a finely-crafted automobile. Only the very rich can afford one — nobles, heads of state, or wealthy leaders of industry. The car promises good looks, quality, quietness, and luxury. The company is usually willing to decorate the interiors of the cars — and occasionally the exteriors — to the buyer's taste.

One of the 50 Rolls-Royces owned by an Indian ruler, the Nizam of Hyderabad, had a body made of solid silver and an interior upholstered in gold brocade. The two Rolls-Royces of the famous newspaper publisher William Randolph Hearst had mirrored interiors, portable bars, tables, and rolltop desks. An heir to the Woolworth fortune had a $1,200 clock and a $3,000 vanity installed in her Rolls-Royce. There have even been bullet-proof Rolls-Royces, as well as models designed to accommodate the owner's wheelchairs.

Charles Rolls, Frederick Royce, and Charles Johnson formed Rolls-Royce Ltd. in 1906. Their first car was a small four-seater with a ten-horsepower, two-cylinder engine. It could reach a top speed of 30 miles per hour. Rolls became interested in flying and was killed in 1910. Johnson died ten years later. Royce then ran the plant alone from his residence in France.

Today the Rolls-Royce is as close to a customized, handmade vehicle as a modern car can be. Each owner is treated as if he or she were a member of the family. The cars are assembled at the rate of 20 per week. Then the finished cars are tested at least three times before they are sold. The two-door Camargue cost $114,000 when it first came out, and owners feel it is worth that kind of money, because it is "the best car in the world."

QUESTIONS

CITING EVIDENCE

1. The author of this article states that the Rolls-Royce is a symbol of luxury. From the list below, which three pieces of evidence are used to support this claim?

    a. The company decorates the interior and exterior of the car according to the buyer's tastes.
    b. Most Rolls-Royces are equipped with fur-trimmed seats.
    c. The Rolls is the most popular automobile with movie stars.
    d. The Nizam of Hyderabad owned a solid silver Rolls.
    e. Some models have included a $3,000 vanity and $1,200 clock.

2. Most of the details in this story describe

    a. American cars designed for economy
    b. the extravagant tastes of William Randolph Hearst
    c. the expensive luxuries of the Rolls-Royce

FACT/OPINION | **3.** For each of the statements below, write in *fact* or *opinion*.

      _____ a. The Rolls-Royce is the best car in the world.

      _____ b. The Rolls is more expensive than it is worth.

      _____ c. Rolls-Royces are assembled at a rate of 20 per week.

ADEQUACY OF INFORMATION | **4.** In the list below, which two pieces of information are presented in the story?

a. Charles Rolls became sole operator of the company after his partners died.

b. New Rolls are tested more than once before they are placed on the market.

c. Most Rolls-Royces are designed for use by handicapped people.

d. The first Rolls-Royce reached a maximum speed of 30 miles per hour.

CONTEXT AND WORD MEANINGS | **5.** The interior of one car was upholstered in gold *brocade.* Check the meaning below for the underlined word in this sentence.

a. coins

b. fabric

c. paint

d. jewelry

AUTHOR'S POINT OF VIEW | **6.** The author of this story believes that

a. Rolls-Royces are great.

b. Rolls-Royces are not what they used to be.

c. Rolls-Royces are a good buy for the average person.

4. Germany's Air Fleet

Before planes made regular Atlantic crossing, magnificent cigar-shaped airships called dirigibles were used to transport air travelers across the ocean. These dirigibles were actually huge balloons made of fabric stretched over a steel skeleton and filled with hydrogen gas. Propellers allowed them to move forward or backward. Between 1928 and 1937 the *Graf Zeppelin,* one of these German dirigibles, made 144 ocean crossings.

In 1937, the huge *Graf Zeppelin* was retired in favor of the new and even larger *Hindenburg.* After ten trips, however, the giant airship exploded and burned at Lakehurst, New Jersey, on May 6, 1937. Thirty-five of the 97 people who were on that ill-fated dirigible died in the huge fire and final crash. Reporters who were covering the landing of the *Hindenburg* were horrified to see the 800-foot dirigible collapse in flames as it attempted to tie up to a mooring tower in a heavy rainstorm. The whole tragic event was captured on motion picture film.

After the *Hindenburg* disaster, a second *Graf Zeppelin* was launched. It was completed in September 1938 and named *Graf Zeppelin II.* This new airship was designed for helium gas, which doesn't explode. Then World War II came along, and Germany was unable to get the helium from America. For a short time, the second *Graf Zeppelin* continued to operate using hydrogen.

In 1940 Germany abandoned its dirigible program. Both the old, decommissioned *Graf Zeppelin* and the new one were dismantled. The steel in their skeletons was used for other purposes. The Zeppelin company produced wartime supplies until it was destroyed by Allied bombers in 1944.

QUESTIONS

SEQUENCE
1. Number each of the airships below according to when they were manufactured. Place a 1 beside the name fo the airship that was made first, a 2 for the second, and a 3 for the third.

   __ *Hindenburg*
   __ *Graf Zeppelin I*
   __ *Graf Zeppelin II*

FACT/OPINION
2. Place an **F** next to the three statements below that are entirely factual.

   ____ a. The first German airship was held aloft by hydrogen gas.
   ____ b. The *Hindenburg* disaster was the worst air tragedy in history.
   ____ c. If scientists could discover a way to make airships more safe, people would enjoy taking short sight-seeing trips in them.
   ____ d. The company that produced the airships was destroyed by bombers during World War II.
   ____ e. The Germans eventually dismantled the *Graf Zeppelins.*

| DETAILS |

3. According to the story, the *Graf Zeppelin II* used hydrogen gas because

    a. it was designed to use hydrogen gas

    b. the ship was easier to maneuver with hydrogen gas

    c. the war prevented Germany from getting helium from America

| DRAWING CONCLUSIONS |

4. From the final paragraph we can conclude that

    a. the Germans decided the dirigibles were not worth a great deal for war purposes

    b. the Germans wanted to build bigger and better dirigibles

    c. the Germans wanted to keep the airships hidden from the Americans

| AUTHOR'S POINT OF VIEW |

5. The author probably wrote this article because

    a. she wanted to point out Germany's weak air defense during World War II

    b. she wanted to show the strained relations between the United States and Germany

    c. she wanted to give a brief history of the German dirigible program

| CONTEXT AND WORD MEANINGS |

6. "Both the old, ***decommissioned*** Graf Zeppelin and the new one were dismantled." In this sentence, the word ***decommissioned*** means

    a. out of use

    b. rebuilt

    c. hydrogen powered

5. Shark Proof

Because the waters off the beaches of South Africa are infested with 17 different species of sharks, crews have now put out heavy nets which fence off 200 miles of oceanfront. Shark encounters with people were first recorded in 1906 at Natal, South Africa. Since then there have been 80 recorded attacks by sharks.

Beginning in 1951, the city of Durban set out vertical nets, called gill nets, off several of its beaches. At first these nets did not attract people back to the beaches. In December 1957 there were so many shark incidents that the month was called Black December. (December is, of course, a summer month in South Africa.) But the nets were extended in 1958, and to help restore confidence, a Shark Board was created. By 1981 there were 200 people involved in shark protection.

The gill nets are 20 feet deep and may be as long as 900 feet (a little more than 1/6th of a mile). Most are made of black polyethylene braid. Black is used because it can't be seen underwater as easily as other colors. The nets are laid on the seabed and secured with anchors. Floating buoys are attached as markers. The nets are set up in two rows parallel to the shore.

The people who police the nets are highly skilled, for they must be able to remove sharks from the nets without being bitten themselves. Each day all the nets are lifted. Any sharks that are tangled in the nets are removed, and the nets are repaired where necessary. Spare nets are kept on hand. Every third week the nets are hauled up and new ones put in place. When taken from the nets, live sharks and other creatures are immediately returned to the ocean.

Shark nets have almost, but not quite, solved the problems of attacks. In February 1980, a man was attacked by a white shark and severely cut. As long as sharks patrol the South African waters there will be need for even better methods of sharkproofing.

QUESTIONS

AUTHOR'S POINT OF VIEW	**1.** Which statement below shows a greater author bias against sharks?

a. Shark encounters with people are fairly rare.
b. Shark attacks on people are fairly rare.

2. Which of these statements shows a greater author bias against sharks?

a. The shark is a killer in his territorial waters.
b. The shark is a hunter in his territorial waters.

FACT/OPINION **3.** "Sharks should all be destroyed." This is a statement of

a. fact
b. probability
c. opinion

CONTEXT AND WORD MEANINGS

4. Fill in the blanks in the following sentences with one of the word choices below so that the sentence makes sense.

a. The shark nets are placed underwater and _____ tightly with anchors.

     suspected   secured   sustained   substance

b. The workers who patrol these nets must be highly _____ so that they aren't bitten.

     slimmed   skinned   slipped   skilled

c. Recently, one man was viciously attacked by a shark and _____ cut.

     severely   simply   secretly   someday

DRAWING CONCLUSIONS

5. The story states that when live sharks and other sea animals are caught in the nets, they are put back into the ocean. With this information, we can conclude that

a. the workers want these animals destroyed

b. the people who patrol the waters aren't concerned with the welfare of the sharks

c. these people don't want to hurt the animals; they merely want to remove them for the safety of others

MAIN IDEA

6. Which of the following pieces of information is *least* important to the story's main idea?

a. In South Africa, special vertical nets are being used to try to control shark attacks.

b. December is a summer month in Africa.

c. Since 1906, there have been 80 recorded shark attacks.

PREDICTING OUTCOMES

7. Once the nets provided better protection, the number of swimmers in that area probably

a. decreased

b. increased

c. stayed the same

6. Express Mail

The Pony Express, which carried the U.S. Mail between the Mississippi Valley and California, has earned a solid place in American legend. Riders sped across western plains, mountains, and deserts, delivering mail across half a continent in only ten days. Almost every trip was an adventure. Yet, the express existed but 19 months and was financially unsound at the end of its time.

The Central Overland Pony Express began on April 3, 1860. Its founder, William H. Russell, thought the service would get him out of financial difficulties. A rider on the Express had to be young, strong, and fearless. Horses were sturdy, grain-fed animals, chosen for stamina. Apparently, the riders were also reliable. The Pony Express lost only one man during its 19 months of operation.

The famous Buffalo Bill Cody was 15 when he became a Pony Express rider. He once rode continually for 322 miles when no relief riders were on hand. The record for the longest single ride, however, goes to "Pony Bob" Haslam, who once rode 380 miles because Indians had raided a number of express stations and scattered the horses.

During its operation, the Pony Express delivered 34,753 pieces of mail. It collected about $1,000 a trip. But this was not enough to pay the expenses of 190 stations, 80 riders, and 500 horses. The sender paid $3.00 for each letter sent, but it cost the company $16.00 to deliver the letter. Then to make matters even worse, the completion of a transcontinental telegraph line in October 1860 made the Pony Express obsolete. The service was terminated on November 20, 1861.

QUESTIONS

ADEQUACY OF INFORMATION

1. Which pieces of information below are presented in the story?

   a. Buffalo Bill Cody founded a Wild West show.
   b. The Pony Express began on April 3, 1860.
   c. A letter cost the sender about $3.00 to send through the Express.
   d. The telegraph was invented by Samuel Morse.
   e. Indians sometimes raided stations.

CONTEXT AND WORD MEANINGS

2. The telegraph made the Pony Express *obsolete.* In this sentence, the italicized word means

   a. out of date
   b. out of touch
   c. out of sight

DETAILS

3. According to the story, what kind of horses were used in the Express?

   a. carriage horses
   b. sturdy horses chosen for stamina
   c. thoroughbred race horses

DRAWING CONCLUSIONS

4. The story tells us that it cost the Express $16.00 to send a letter, while the sender paid only $3.00. With this information, we can conclude that

    a. the Pony Express made its owners rich very quickly
    b. the company charged its customers too much to send mail
    c. the company lost money

FACT/OPINION

5. Some of the statements below are facts, some are opinions, and some are probabilities. In the space to the left, place an **F** if it is a statement of fact, an **O** if the statement is an opinion, and a **P** if the statement is a probability.

    _____ a. Every trip was a wonderful adventure for the riders.
    _____ b. The Pony Express would not work well today.
    _____ c. The founder of the company was William H. Russell.
    _____ d. The Indians raided the Pony Express stations.
    _____ e. The Express operated for 19 months.
    _____ f. "Pony Bob" Haslam was the greatest express rider.

7. The Journeys of the Caribou

It is autumn in Alaska. The snows have already begun. In the treeless grazing lands of the north, the caribou are moving south. These New World relatives of the reindeer make long journeys south every year when winter approaches.

The cold does not bother them because of their thick coats. Neither does the snow. The name *caribou* comes from an Indian word meaning "pawing," and that is what the caribou do to get their food. They paw away the snow to find moss and grass underneath. But they cannot paw through the ice that will soon cover the ground. And so they must move south.

Caribou are expert travelers in the snow. They move in single file, each animal stepping in the tracks of the one before it. Eventually, after traveling hundreds of miles, they reach the edge of the great forest of the north. There they will spend the winter.

When spring comes, the caribou must return north. This spring migration is the most pressing journey. Female caribou need to get back to the home range to have their calves. When the journey begins, lakes and streams are still frozen. Storms still rage. After a long winter, the caribou are like scarecrows from months of very limited food. Why do they begin to migrate in mid-March? No one knows for sure. The increasing daylight may have something to do with it.

The greatest danger on the journey north is from wolves. They attack caribou at the head and neck, not about the legs as many people believe. A pack of five or ten hungry wolves will often completely devour a caribou in two days.

In the summer the caribou are pestered by mosquitoes. They often run about seeking escape from the insects. It is the end of summer or the beginning of fall before they really can begin to fatten up. During this period they also grow a fine coat and a new set of antlers. They are then ready to breed and to start on south to their winter home in the forest.

QUESTIONS

CONTEXT AND WORD MEANINGS

1. The spring migration is the most ***pressing*** journey for the caribou. In this sentence, the italicized word means

a. heavy
b. flat
c. important

DETAILS

2. According to the story, which two of the following are the greatest dangers to the caribou?

    a. snow
    b. cold
    c. wolves
    d. mosquitoes
    e. ice

SEQUENCE

3. At the left is a list of events that take place along the caribou's annual journey. The seasons in which these events take place are listed on the right. Match.

    ____ The animals must paw the ground to find food.   a. summer
    ____ Mosquitoes torment the caribou.   b. winter
    ____ Females increase the herds with new-born calves.   c. spring

MAIN IDEA

4. The main point of this story is that

    a. caribou undergo annual journeys filled with hardships
    b. increasing daylight may account for the spring migration of the caribou
    c. the caribou get their name from an old Indian word meaning "pawing"

PREDICTING OUTCOMES

5. Based on the information in the story, which of the following would be most likely to happen if there were less ice during the winter?

    a. The spring migration would be even more difficult.
    b. The caribou would begin the spring stronger and healthier.
    c. The animals would have to paw more than ever to find food.

DRAWING CONCLUSIONS

6. Based on the information in the story, you could conclude

    a. the caribou cannot survive in very cold temperatures
    b. mosquitoes prove to be the greatest danger on the caribou's journey
    c. the caribou are strong animals

8. The Oracle of Delphi

People have always wanted to see into the future. In ancient Greece, people who wanted to know the future went to a holy place at Delphi, located on the slopes of Mt. Parnassus in central Greece. There, priestesses, called Pythia, uttered predictions called oracles while they were in a state of frenzy. The oracles were supposed to be the words of the god Apollo, who expressed the will of his father, Zeus.

The oracle at Delphi was older than the Greeks themselves. Around 1500 B. C., the priests of an earlier people established an oracle there. Later, about 1100 B. C., the invading Greeks took it over and used it as an oracle for their own god, Apollo.

Over the centuries, the oracle at Delphi proved highly accurate. Delphi's reputation grew. Grateful people bestowed wealth on the temple. In the 6th Century B. C., the temple received more wealth than it could spend, so treasure houses were constructed to hold the gold and silver.

The predictions of the oracle were often accurate, but equally often they had double meanings. In some cases, the oracle ignored the question. A man named Battus sought to have his stuttering cured, and the priestess said he would found an empire. He did establish the empire, but continued his stuttering!

The most famous, and one of the most misleading, of the Delphic predictions was the one given to King Croesus of Lydia. In 550 B. C. he was preparing to invade the Persian Empire. He asked about his chances of victory. The oracle told him, "Croesus will destroy a great empire." He invaded Persia, and was beaten and imprisoned. The oracle had told the truth. Croesus had destroyed a great empire — his own!

QUESTIONS

MAIN IDEA

1. This story is mainly about

   a. the gods the Greeks worshipped
   b. the predictions made by the oracle at Delphi
   c. the life of King Croesus

ADEQUACY OF INFORMATION

2. Which of the following pieces of information is *not* included in this story?

   a. The oracle was established about 1500 B. C.
   b. Apollo was the Greek god of the sun.
   c. The man named Battus stuttered.

DETAILS

3. The story tells us that the priestesses uttered predictions while

   a. the priests burned incense in the temple
   b. Apollo chanted ancient songs
   c. they were in a state of frenzy

4. Based on the information in the story, which three of the words below best describe the Delphic oracle?

    a. accurate
    b. silent
    c. misleading
    d. wealthy
    e. wrong

DRAWING CONCLUSIONS

5. Based on the information presented in the final paragraph, we can conclude that

    a. the oracle sometimes gave confusing information
    b. the oracle lied to King Croesus
    c. the oracle wanted King Croesus to conquer Persia

SEQUENCE

6. Using the time line below, match the letter of the date to the correct event at the left. Write the letter in the blank next to each event.

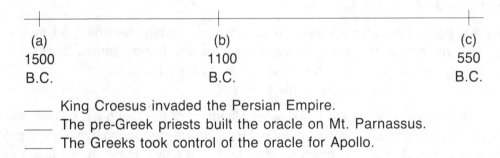

(a) 1500 B.C.   (b) 1100 B.C.   (c) 550 B.C.

____ King Croesus invaded the Persian Empire.
____ The pre-Greek priests built the oracle on Mt. Parnassus.
____ The Greeks took control of the oracle for Apollo.

9. Conqueror of Everest

On June 2, 1953, the coronation of Queen Elizabeth II of England took place. Also on that day Edmund Hillary was knighted, for he had recently ascended Mt. Everest. He was the first man to stand on top of the highest peak in the world!

Sir Edmund was the son of a New Zealand bookkeeper. Except for a school skiing trip to 9,000-foot Ruapehu Mountain when he was 16, he had no experience with mountains until he was 20. That year, he visited New Zealand's Mt. Cook National Park, though not with the idea of climbing Mt. Cook. But one evening two men came into the ski lodge looking exuberant after their climb to the summit of the 12,000-foot peak. The next day, Hillary hired a guide and made the climb. From then on he spent his holidays climbing.

In 1950, Hillary went to England to meet mountain climbers and climb with English mountaineers. He was included in a planned 1953 expedition to Everest. Britain had had earlier expeditions to Mt. Everest in 1922, 1924, 1936, and 1938. In the last of these, climbers had reached the 28,000-foot level, about 100 feet below the top. But no one had yet climbed all the way to the summit.

The 1953 expedition was led by John Hunt. Hillary and his guide Tenzing were chosen to try the climb to the top if a first pair of climbers failed. The first pair returned to camp covered with ice and exhausted. At 28,000 feet Hillary and Tenzing camped for the night. The next day, after many difficulties, they reached the top. Their path was no longer up, but down on all sides!

Since climbing Mt. Everest, Hillary has taken an active interest in the region surrounding the great mountain. He has helped build 17 schools for the Sherpas, the local people to whom his guide Tenzing belonged. He has also helped to form Sugarmantha National Park on the border between Nepal and Tibet.

QUESTIONS

SEQUENCE 1. Review the events as they took place in the story. Then cross out one of the words in each of the parentheses to make each statement correct.

    a. Sir Edmund Hillary climbed Mt. Everest (before, after) he visited Ruapehu Mountain.

    b. He helped build Sherpa schools (before, after) he conquered Everest.

    c. He climbed Mt. Cook (before, after) he made the Everest climb.

CITING EVIDENCE 2. What evidence can you give to support the statement, "Hillary became active in improving the region surrounding the mountain"?

_____

_____

DETAILS

3. Who accompanied Hillary to the top of Mt. Everest?

    a. Tenzing
    b. John Hunt
    c. Queen Elizabeth

DRAWING CONCLUSIONS

4. We can conclude from the final paragraph of the story that Hillary

    a. was interested only in climbing Everest
    b. has a strong liking for the area around Mt. Everest
    c. remains uncaring towards the Sherpa people

ADEQUACY OF INFORMATION

5. Which items of information below are presented in the story?

    a. Hillary's father was a bookkeeper.
    b. Hillary was knighted for his famous climb.
    c. Hillary lived with a Sherpa family after his climb of Everest.
    d. Other expeditions had been lost on the mountain before Hillary made his climb.
    e. Hillary was originally from New Zealand.

CONTEXT AND WORD MEANINGS

6. The men looked *exuberant* after their successful climb. In this sentence, the italicized word means

    a. exhausted
    b. frozen
    c. joyful
    d. dejected

10. Lapps

The air is clean and dry. For a few days in summer the sun never sets, but for a few days in winter it never rises. The unspoiled beauty and isolation is intensified by the winter cold. Exposed flesh is numb in a few seconds, nostrils tingle, and bare hands stick to metal. Where is this hostile land? It is in Scandinavia, about 1,400 miles from the North Pole. The people who inhabit this frigid land are Lapps.

The Lapps — whose name for themselves is "Sami" — live in the very northern parts of Norway, Sweden, Finland, and part of Russia. There are about 30,000 Lapps in this stark land. Most are herders who follow reindeer on migration routes and live far from the centers of civilization. They speak their own language, live in tents during the migration, and wear red stocking caps, curled-up-at-the-toe moccasins, and dark coats with colorful embroidery.

The Lapp way of life is unique, and so Norway, Sweden, and Finland have established the Nordic Sami Institute to preserve and protect their cultural heritage. Since Norway is the home of two-thirds of the Lapps, Norway pays $500,000 per year into their institute. The Norwegian government also provides money for special educational programs. It offers Lapp studies as well as reindeer research at its national universities.

But Lapp life is changing. In recent years, more and more Laplanders have become reindeer breeders — more like farmers than herders. Hard-working reindeer breeders may make up to $20,000 a year — as much as most people do in the cities. Reindeer meat is in great demand in Scandinavia. Reindeer meat sells in the cities for about $3.00 per pound.

Lapps are settling in towns, too. In the town of Kautokeino, 250 miles north of the Arctic Circle, there are nearly 3,000 Lapps. They drive new Toyota and Ford cars as well as snowmobiles made in Japan and Canada. They watch television. The Norwegian Lapps are required to know the Norwegian language, as well as their own, and they can, therefore, understand Norwegian TV.

Some Lapps no longer stay home all year around. They take foreign vacations and seem especially to like the Canary Islands. In one very cold winter, many took trips to Paris and the French Riviera. Nevertheless, many older Lapps feel that their biggest problem today is to learn to minimize the undesirable effects of modern life.

QUESTIONS

ADEQUACY OF INFORMATION

1. Which two situations below show probable cause-effect relationships?

    a. The Lapps speak their own language, so they raise reindeer.
    b. The Lapland areas are bitterly cold, and exposed flesh becomes numb in seconds.
    c. Laplanders now drive popular automobiles and take vacations to warm places; some older Lapps fear the effects of modern life.
    d. The sun sets very abruptly in Lapland, and some Lapps make as much money as city dwellers.

DETAILS

2. Most of the Lapland population lives in

    a. Norway
    b. Sweden
    c. Finland

MAIN IDEA

3. The main idea of Paragraph 3 is that

    a. reindeer research is important in Norwegian universities
    b. the government funds special education programs
    c. Norway provides special funds and programs for Lapps

PREDICTING OUTCOMES

4. Based on the information in the final two paragraphs of the story, the Lapps will probably

    a. become less isolated in the future as they travel and acquire modern things
    b. return to a more primitive lifestyle
    c. avoid travel and contact with other countries

CONTEXT AND WORD MEANINGS

5. The Laplander's environment is cold and hostile. Exposed skin can be harmed by the *frigid* air. In this sentence, the italicized word means

    a. windy
    b. freezing
    c. cool

DRAWING CONCLUSIONS

6. Paragraph 4 leads us to conclude that

    a. more and more Lapps are working in industrial areas
    b. farming is the main source of income for most Lapps
    c. reindeer breeding has become a high income occupation for Lapps